Official Soccer Rules Illustrated

by Stanley Lover

Foreword by Michel Zen-Ruffinen
General Secretary, FIFA

Illustrations by Joe Colquhoun and Stanley Lover

Including

The Laws of the Game and Decisions
of the International Football Association Board

Reproduction authorized by the
Federation Internationale de Football Association

All rights reserved by FIFA

ALSO BY STANLEY LOVER:

Soccer Rules Explained
Soccer Laws Illustrated
Soccer Match Control
Soccer Judge
Soccer and Its Rules
Illustrated Soccer Quiz Book
Fair Play Guide
You are the Ref!

This book is available in quantity at special discounts for your
group or organization. For more information, contact:

Triumph Books
601 South LaSalle Street
Suite 500
Chicago, Illinois 60605
(312) 939-3330
Fax (312) 663-3557

Cover photo: Phil Stephens

Book design by Eileen Wagner

ISBN 1-57243-330-2

KICKOFF TO FINAL WHISTLE

"The People's Game"

SOCCER—"THE PEOPLE'S GAME"

Soccer has been described as "The People's Game" because it appeals to millions bound together in a world soccer family. It is a joy to play because each player can express personal skills in an exciting sport. It is a joy to watch because the ball is always visible and the play easy to follow.

Soccer is at its best when a game flows from goal to goal and when players display their skills in a spirit of fair play, respecting opponents, officials, and faithful supporters while creating a pleasurable experience.

To make the most of each soccer game requires a basic knowledge of the rules. Players need to know what is fair and unfair to avoid offenses which stop the play, give the ball to the opponents, and frustrate their skills' potential. Coaches and club officials need to know enough to set correct disciplines on and off the field. For parents and friends of soccer, a basic knowledge will help them understand and enjoy "The People's Game" better.

The purpose of this book is to provide a visual link between the legalistic text of the official rules and the excitement of actual play. The complete and formal Laws of the Game are included for readers who wish to know more.

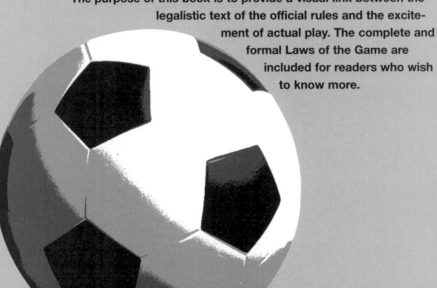

FOREWORD

The rules of any sport should be clear and easy to apply. In soccer we are fortunate to have just seventeen, founded on basic concepts which have stood the test of time in life and in play. Our set of simple rules has established soccer as the world's most popular sport, giving pleasure to all members of the family. Even so, where individual passions are touched, we are drawn into discussion, controversy, and disagreement about how these rules are, or should be, applied.

It is FIFA's endless quest to achieve consistency of interpretation and application of all the formal Laws of the Game. Perfection will remain elusive, as in so many things in life, for the play is guided on the field by human beings—Referees—with all of the individualistic quirks that this implies. Whatever differences of opinion may arise, FIFA holds fast to the sporting ethic that the decisions of a neutral arbiter, on facts connected with the play, are final.

To reduce areas of controversy, FIFA welcomes publications such as this one by an acknowledged expert on the game and its rules. It is a visual link between the written rules and the play. It is a guide, not only to the application of the Rules but also to the roles of all members of the soccer family on how to safeguard the true values of Fair Play in our sport.

Fair Play is Better Play.

Michel Zen-Ruffinen
General Secretary, FIFA

v

PREFACE

Over 200 countries are members of FIFA, which administrates the game of soccer. In truth, soccer is the World Game. It attracts players of all ages because it is a simple and enjoyable activity. It requires minimum and inexpensive equipment and all the things which the physically fit like to do are implicit in the game.

Running, jumping, bodily contact, and, above all, kicking an object are all part of a sporting "war game" where the object is to capture (and recapture) the enemy's stronghold—his goal.

Just as there are Rules of War to limit excesses and which should be honored (but sometimes aren't), so there are Rules of the Game which should be observed (but sometimes aren't) to ensure the safety of the players and provide the maximum enjoyment for them and spectators alike.

Soccer has been played in its present form since 1863 but the rules have changed very little in their basic principles. Most of the changes in detail, particularly in recent years, have tended to recognize the increasing pace of play and advances in technology. Although players and spectators have a general grasp of the rules there is no doubt that a better understanding of their purpose and application will add to the pleasures of the game. Conversely, a poor or mistaken interpretation often provokes unjust criticism of referees' decisions with consequent loss of enjoyment.

Referees make fewer errors than is generally supposed. They study hard to apply the spirit of the rules, as well as the letter, to enable games to be played in a sporting climate. This book will help towards a better appreciation of the game, its rules, and the part all soccer people can play to keep it a clean and healthy sport.

Ken Aston M.B.E.
International Referee, past Chairman, FIFA Referees' Committee, and Member of the International Football Association Board

THE SPIRIT OF THE GAME

Soccer is more than a simple game. It is an emotional experience.

The mechanics of the play amount to the movement of a ball, about the size of a man's head, between two targets set some distance apart. But, in the course of just one game, the whole range of human emotions from the depths of despair to utter joy can be touched in the hearts of those who play or watch.

Somewhere in these emotions lies the key to the Spirit of the Game, a term often mentioned but rarely defined. To merely present in these pages a series of illustrations of the written rules without considering the spirit in which they are intended to be applied would offer an unfinished story.

The spirit in which the game should be played was considered more important than the written rule by the nineteenth century founders of the game. A few rules, or Laws as they were styled, were set down to regulate the physical play, but not a word was included on the principles or ethics to be observed. In those days it was not necessary to write down a code of conduct. After all, the game as we know it today was devised by intelligent, respected men steeped in the codes of ethics and gentlemanly conduct imposed by the strict era of Queen Victoria of England.

Much wisdom was included in those few early rules because the game has remained practically unchanged for over 130 years. Those early and subsequent legislators have carefully guarded the inner soul of soccer when considering alterations.

A close look at the reasoning behind the written rules provides three important clues to the interpretation of the Spirit of the Game in the form of three basic principles:

EQUAL OPPORTUNITY. All players must have an equal opportunity to demonstrate individual skills without unfair interference from opponents. Physical size or brute strength are not essential elements for success. Players of small stature can show their skills, by quick reactions and balance, alongside others whose assets include height and strength. Many players of small physique have achieved world fame by showing their exciting skills.

SAFETY. Playing the game involves physical contact which can be tough. The rules provide a certain protection for players in specifying safety features for game components, equipment worn, and injury care, plus limitations to physical challenges for the ball.

ENJOYMENT. The rules are clear on describing unfair play and acts of misconduct which destroy skill and the pleasure of playing or watching the game. The purpose of the written rules is to provide a stimulating and healthy sport in which people of all ages can experience the maximum enjoyment.

Summarizing then, the basic principles of the Spirit of the Game are simply: **EQUALITY—SAFETY—ENJOYMENT**

The governing body for the Laws of the Game, the International Football Association Board, receives many suggestions to improve the game and change the laws. The following statement, issued by the IFAB after the annual meeting in 1968, remains valid in today's game:

"It is the belief of the Board that the Spirit in which the Game is played is of paramount importance and that changes in the Laws, to improve the Game as a spectacle, are of little value if 'fair play' is not universally observed."

FAIR PLAY IN SPORT

DEFINITION Fair play in sport is a code of conduct which respects both the written and unwritten rules of play. Opponents are accepted as partners in sport.

Fair play is expressed through spontaneous actions which applaud sporting excellence, which show concern for opponents in distress, which acknowledge defeat with dignity and victory with humility.

Sport with fair play enriches the quality of life.

—**Stanley F. Lover**

THE GAME

Soccer (a contraction of Association Football) is a team game played by people of all ages. It is played for pure enjoyment in friendly games or competitively in matches between teams in organized tournaments.

COMPONENTS Essential components are players, a ball, and space.

OBJECT The object of the game is to combine the skills of the players in a team effort to move the ball through the opponents' goal to score a goal.

MATCH RESULT The team scoring the highest number of goals wins the match. If both teams score an equal number of goals, or if no goals are scored, the match is drawn.

METHOD OF PLAY To achieve a score each team attacks the opponents' goal, generally by a series of passing movements of the ball, using any part of the body (except hands or arms) to put the ball through the goal. Each team has a goalkeeper who is allowed to use hands to protect the goal.

RULES OF PLAY Matches are regulated by the Laws of the Game as decided by the International Football Association Board. These may be modified within approved limits for tournament play. Players are required to understand and respect the official Laws of the Game and any special tournament rules.

THE REFEREE To ensure that matches are played in accordance with the Laws and tournament rules a Referee is appointed to supervise the play inside the field. Assistant Referees, when available, supervise certain aspects of play from outside of the field boundary lines.

DECISIONS OF THE REFEREE The decisions of the Referee regarding facts connected with play are final.

THE GAME OF SOCCER

DEFINITION OF TERMS USED IN THE LAWS OF THE GAME

ADVANTAGE At an offense the Referee may allow play to continue if it is to the advantage of the non-offending team.

CAUTION A formal warning against further unfair play or unsporting behavior. Indicated by a yellow card shown by the Referee.

COACH A team official who may convey tactical instructions to the players during a match.

DANGEROUS PLAY Any action, considered by the Referee to be dangerous to another player, which is not a listed offense.

FREE KICK "The privilege of Kicking the Ball, without obstruction, in such a manner as the Kicker may see fit." (Original definition of 1863 which remains valid in the modern game.)

GOALKEEPER An identified player in each team permitted to touch the ball with the hands, inside the penalty area, to defend the goal.

HANDLING Deliberate use of the hand or arm to influence the movement of the ball by a player other than a goalkeeper.

IMPEDING An offense when a player who is not playing the ball impedes the progress of an opponent by interposing his body between the opponent and the ball.

MISCONDUCT Any act of misbehavior contrary to the letter and spirit of the Laws of the Game.

OFFSIDE POSITION A player is in an offside position if he is nearer to his opponents' goal line than the ball, unless he (a) is in his own half, or (b) is level with the second-to-last opponent, or (c) is level with the last two opponents. It is not an offense to be in an offside position.

OFFSIDE An offense when a player is in an offside position and is judged, by the Referee, to be interfering with the play, with an opponent, or gaining an advantage.

SCORING A team scores a goal when the ball passes through the opposing team's goal in compliance with the Laws.

TACKLING A challenge made with the foot, either from the front or the side, to play the ball while it is in the possession of an opponent.

x

SECTION 1

COMPONENTS

*FOUR ESSENTIAL
ELEMENTS TO START
ANY MATCH*

COMPONENTS

A game of soccer does not need elaborate equipment. In kick-about games it is not even necessary to have a ball! Many children make do with objects, varying from bundles of rags tied with string, cartons, and cans, to paper cups, shoes, and caps!

What imagination! And what fun! No need for rules in these games. The playing area is any available space, be it in the streets, on a beach, on a flat roof, or inside a home.

The formal Laws of the Game are for soccer players who want to play in friendly team games or in organized matches in competitions.

Much care has been devoted to setting down the basic components common to all matches, no matter where they may be played.

Standard equipment is intended to minimize elements of danger and yet encourage maximum effort.

The first four laws detail the essentials—the playing field, the ball, the players, and their equipment.

3

LAW 1
THE FIELD OF PLAY

- Soccer is played on a rectangular field to encourage the flow of play between the main targets, i.e. the goals.

- The size of the field may be varied between given limits according to the space available. However, the named areas within the boundaries are of fixed dimensions.

- The field is divided into two equal halves.

- Goal nets are advisable but not compulsory.

4

The field of play, showing the penalty, goal, and corner areas shaded.

THE FIELD OF PLAY

- The size of the goal is related to the physical capability of the goalkeeper to defend the goal and to demand skill from attacking players to score.

- The goalposts are white in color so they can be seen easily.

The Goal

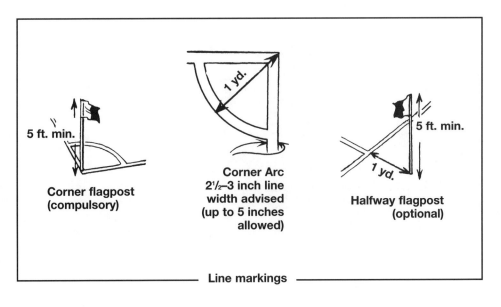

Line markings

LAW 1
THE FIELD OF PLAY

Q If, during a game, a crossbar is broken, may it be replaced?

A The use of a rope to replace the crossbar is not permitted.
(*Decision 1*)

6

● Flagposts shorter than 5 feet (1.50 m.) are dangerous.

LAW 2
THE BALL

- A spherical ball is chosen for the game of soccer because it truly reflects the skill of the player in kicking, heading, controlling, or moving it in any manner permitted by the rules.

- Its size, weight, pressure, and materials used in manufacture are required to meet rigid FIFA standards.

Q Are all matches played with the same size ball?

A No. A smaller ball is advised for players under sixteen years of age and for young women players.

Q May the ball be changed during a game?

A "The ball may not be changed during the match without the authority of the Referee."

Advice

It is advisable to choose a match ball inflated to suit the conditions of play. Generally, a soft ball is preferred on a hard surface and a harder ball on a soft or very wet surface.

7

LAW 3

THE PLAYERS

- In every match there are two teams each having not more than eleven players on the field. Where competition rules permit, up to three substitutes may be used. In non-competition games up to five substitutes may be used.

- One player of each team is a goalkeeper with the privilege of handling the ball within his team's penalty area.

Q A team starts a match with only ten players. The eleventh player arrives at the commencement of the second half. May he join his team?

A Yes, provided that the Referee is advised. If the game is in progress the player must wait for a signal from the Referee.

"A match may not start if either team consists of fewer than seven players."

LAW 3
THE PLAYERS

Q May a player who has had to leave the field for treatment of an injury return to his team?

A Yes, after receiving a signal from the Referee.

Q A goalkeeper is injured and wishes to change places with another player. Is this permitted?

A Yes, at any time, provided that the Referee is advised when the change is to be made and that play has been stopped.

LAW 3
THE PLAYERS

Q What is the procedure for a substitute to join the game?

A
- There is normal stoppage of play;
- the Referee is notified;
- the outgoing player has left the field;
- the Referee signals the new player to enter the field;
- the new player enters at the halfway line.

Q If a player is dismissed from the game for misconduct, may his place be taken by a substitute (No. 12)?

A A player who has been dismissed *after* a match has started cannot be replaced.

"A player who has been sent off *before* the kickoff may be replaced only by one of the named substitutes."

LAW 4

THE PLAYERS' EQUIPMENT

Shirt

Shorts

Stockings

Shinguards

- The main points of this law are *safety* for the players and *correct presentation* on the field of play.

- The basic compulsory equipment includes shinguards to protect the player's legs. In addition it is the player's responsibility not to wear anything which could be dangerous to himself or to any other player. To assist players in obtaining a secure foothold, footwear incorporating bars or studs is permitted but these must be checked regularly to minimize the element of danger to other players.

Footwear

11

- Goalkeepers must be clearly identified by wearing colors which avoid possible confusion with other players, the Referee, and Assistant Referees.

Q Can any action be taken if a player advises the Referee that an injury has been caused by the studs on an opponent's boot?

A The Referee has power to examine players' footwear at any time and to instruct any player to leave the match to correct items considered to be dangerous.

LAW 4
THE PLAYERS' EQUIPMENT

● The Referee may require a player to remove a ring or any other article which could cause injury.

Q May a player wear glasses during a match?

A The Laws do not prohibit glasses. The obvious danger to the wearer, and to other players, should be clearly understood before the match commences.

Q A player decides to play without any footwear. Is this permitted?

A No. Compulsory equipment includes footwear.

LAW 4
THE PLAYERS' EQUIPMENT

Q When a player has had to leave the field to correct some item of equipment, how may he rejoin the game?

A The player must wait for a stoppage in the game before reporting to the Referee, who will then examine the player's equipment and satisfy himself that it is in order.

13

Q What would happen if a player who has left the field with the Referee's permission to correct dangerous equipment rejoined the game without waiting for play to be stopped?

A The Referee is required to caution the player (Law 12, caution offense No. 6). An indirect free kick is awarded to the opposing team.

SECTION 2

RULES OF PLAY

BASIC PROCEDURES

RULES OF PLAY

Now that we have the essential components, the game can begin.

Like for any other sport, the rules of play for soccer deal with the method of playing the game—how to start and restart, timing, how to score, etc.

Nine of the official laws deal with these rules of play.

17

LAW 7
THE DURATION OF THE MATCH

- The normal period of play is 90 minutes, made up of two equal periods of 45 minutes. These periods may be slightly reduced for young players. Where competition rules allow, extra time may be played in the event of there being no result at the end of the normal period.

18

- When the game is delayed to allow an injured player to be examined or removed from the field, the Referee will make allowance to compensate for the amount of time lost.

- The Referee is required to make allowances for time lost during substitutions, dealing with offending players, or any other reason at the Referee's discretion.

LAW 7
THE DURATION OF THE MATCH

Q As the Referee is about to signal the end of play a defender handles the ball in his own penalty area. What action must the Referee take?

A A penalty kick must be awarded.

The Referee has authority to extend playing time to allow a penalty kick to be taken at the end of a normal period.

Note:

If a defender denies an opponent an obvious goal opportunity (as here) the Referee is required, by Law 12, to dismiss the offending player.

19

Q At the end of the first period of play the visiting team's captain asks the Referee to commence the second period without an interval so that his team can start their return journey as early as possible. Would this be in order?

A The law entitles players to an interval at halftime not to exceed 15 minutes. There is no minimum. If all players agree to a brief interval the Referee would be in order to consent unless a competition rule insists on a minimum period.

LAW 8
STARTING AND RESTARTING PLAY

- Each team defends one half of the field. The toss of a coin decides which team chooses the goal it wishes to attack. The other team will have first possession of the ball at the kickoff.

- After the halftime interval the teams change ends. The second period of the match is started by a kickoff, taken by the team which did not start play in the first period.

- Play is also restarted with a kickoff after a goal has been scored.

- To restart play after a temporary halt for any cause not mentioned elsewhere in the Laws, the Referee will drop the ball at the appropriate place.

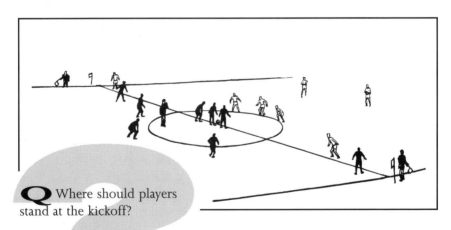

Q Where should players stand at the kickoff?

A Every player is in his own half of the field. Players of the team opposing the kickoff remain not less than 10 yards from the ball until it is kicked and moves forward.

STARTING AND RESTARTING PLAY

Q At a kickoff the ball is kicked directly into the opponents' goal. Is this a goal?

A Yes. A goal may be scored directly from a kickoff. (1997 law change)

21

Q May a player kick the ball before it touches the ground when it is being dropped by the Referee?

A No. The ball is not in play until it touches the ground. In this case the Referee would drop the ball again.

LAW 9
BALL IN AND OUT OF PLAY

● The boundary lines, i.e. goal lines and touchlines, contain the game within a reasonable area to encourage the flow of play between the goal targets.

● The ball is out of play, and the game brought to a halt, when the whole of the ball has crossed over a boundary line, either on the ground or in the air.

● The lines belong to the areas of which they are the boundaries.

22

Out of play

Touchline (or Goal Line)

Out

In play

Field

LAW 9
BALL IN AND OUT OF PLAY

Q Should play be stopped if the ball strikes the Referee?

A No. Law 9 states that the ball is in play if "it rebounds from either the Referee or an Assistant Referee when they are on the field of play."

In the case shown here a goal would be awarded.

Q If the ball goes over the goal line but is caught by the goalkeeper who is standing in the field of play, must the game be stopped?

A Yes, if the ball has passed completely over the goal line. The position of the goalkeeper does not alter this fact.

LAW 10
METHOD OF SCORING

- "The team scoring the greater number of goals during a match is the winner. If both teams score an equal number of goals, or if no goals are scored, the match is drawn."

- To score a goal, the whole of the ball must pass over the goal line, between the posts, and under the crossbar.

- If the ball wholly crosses the goal line but returns into the field of play, the goal is valid.

24

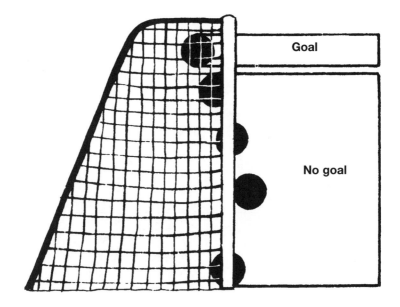

Goal

No goal

METHOD OF SCORING

Q If the ball is about to enter the goal but is deflected by a dog (or spectator), can the Referee award a goal?

A The revised laws of 1997 do not refer to this eventuality but the traditional interpretation (in accordance with the spirit of the law) is not to allow a goal and to restart play by dropping the ball.

25

Q Would a goal be scored if a goalkeeper, standing in his own penalty area, throws the ball with the aid of a strong wind into his opponents' goal without any other player touching the ball?

A Yes. This is the only way in which an attacking player can score by the use of the hands.

FREE KICKS

● Free kicks are awarded by the Referee to penalize infringements of the Laws. "Free" means "free from interference by players of the offending team." They must not approach nearer to the ball than the limits imposed in the Laws until the ball has been kicked into play.

● There are two types of free kick:

(a) Direct—from which a goal can be scored against the opposing team when the ball passes directly into the goal;

(b) Indirect—from which a goal can only be scored if the ball is touched or played by a player of either team after it is kicked into play and before it enters the goal.

26

Ball stationary

Opponents at least 10 yd. from the ball

Teammates may stand nearer than 10 yd.

Position of Players at a Free Kick

FREE KICKS

Q If a defending player takes a direct free kick from outside his penalty area and kicks the ball past his own goalkeeper into the goal, what would be the correct decision?

A The Referee would award a corner kick to the attacking team because a goal can only be scored against the offending team from a direct free kick.

27

Q How do players and spectators know if the free kick is direct or indirect?

A When the Referee awards an indirect free kick he signals it by raising his arm. This signal precedes the blowing of the whistle for the free kick to be taken; no such signal is given in the case of a direct free kick.

If the ball goes directly into the opponents' goal from an indirect free kick, a goal kick is awarded to the defending team.

LAW 13
FREE KICKS

Q May the defending players stand less than 10 yards from the ball at any time?

A Only when an indirect free kick is to be taken from a position less than 10 yards away from the goal. Defenders may stand on the goal line between the posts.

Q Can defending players move nearer than 10 yards when the signal is given?

A Not until the ball has been kicked into play.

Note:

At a free kick the kicker must not touch the ball a second time before it has touched another player.

LAW 13
FREE KICKS

Q If the defending team is awarded a free kick outside of their own penalty area may the ball be kicked to the goalkeeper?

A Yes, but if the goalkeeper touches the ball with his hands inside the penalty area, an indirect free kick (Law 12) is awarded to the opposing team.

29

Q From an indirect free kick the ball strikes the crossbar, hits the goalkeeper, and bounces over the goal line. Would this be a goal?

A Yes, because the ball was last played by a player other than the kicker before it entered the goal.

LAW 14
PENALTY KICK

- A penalty kick is an important award to punish any of the ten offenses listed in Law 12 when committed by a player within his own team's penalty area.

- Law 14 describes the requirements for taking a penalty kick. These include restrictions on the conduct of the kicker, the goalkeeper, and the other players.

- Playing time may be extended to allow a penalty kick to be taken (Law 7). The Referee decides when the penalty kick has been completed.

- "The Players other than the kicker are located:
  - inside the field of play
  - outside the penalty area
  - behind the penalty mark
  - at least 10 yards (9.15 m) from the penalty mark."

- The goalkeeper stands on the goal line between the posts.

Behind the Penalty Mark

Positions of Players at a Penalty Kick

PENALTY KICK

Q The Referee has given the signal for the penalty to be taken, but before the ball is kicked, a defender moves into the penalty area. What is the correct procedure?

A The Referee will not delay the kick. If a goal is scored it will be allowed. If a goal is not scored the kick must be retaken.

Q What would happen if a player of each team encroached into the penalty area or within 10 yards of the penalty mark before the ball is in play?

A The penalty kick must be retaken.

LAW 14

PENALTY KICK

Q Is the goalkeeper allowed to move before the ball is kicked?

A Yes, along the goal line but not towards the ball.

32

Q Would a goal be allowed if the ball was to strike the crossbar or goalpost and return to the kicker who then kicked it into the goal?

A A goal would not be allowed because the kicker must not play the ball a second time until it has been touched by another player. The Referee would award an indirect free kick against the kicker.

Q The Referee has extended time to allow a penalty kick to be taken. If the ball rebounds from the goalkeeper to the kicker, who scores and will the goal be allowed?

A No. The game ends the moment the goalkeeper prevents the ball from entering the goal.

LAW 15
THROW-IN

- When the ball passes over a touchline the game is restarted by a throw-in awarded to the team opposite to that of the player who last touched the ball.

- A goal cannot be scored direct from a throw-in.

Correct throw-in.
Facing field of play.
Both feet on ground.
On or behind line.

Incorrect.
Only one foot on ground.

Incorrect.
Only one hand throwing ball.

Correct.
Both hands throwing ball.

LAW 15
THROW-IN

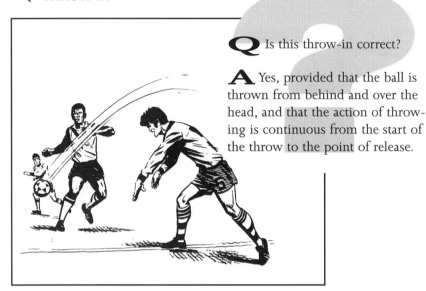

Q Is this throw-in correct?

A Yes, provided that the ball is thrown from behind and over the head, and that the action of throwing is continuous from the start of the throw to the point of release.

Q A defender takes a throw-in and throws the ball back to his goalkeeper. The ball goes directly into the goal before the goalkeeper touches it. Is it a goal?

A No. A goal cannot be scored directly from a throw-in. In this case a corner kick is awarded to the opposing team.

GOAL KICK

- When a player of the attacking team plays the ball over the goal line, excluding the portion between the goalposts, the defending team is awarded a goal kick.

- The ball is not in play until it has been kicked directly out of the penalty area. A goal may be scored direct from a goal kick.

Correct Goal Kick

- The ball is kicked from any point within the goal area when all opponents are outside of the penalty area.

LAW 16
GOAL KICK

● If the ball is played before it passes outside of the penalty area the goal kick is retaken.

Q If the ball is kicked over the goal line before it has cleared the penalty area, should the Referee award a corner kick?

A Because the ball was not in play when it crossed the goal line, the goal kick must be retaken.

LAW 17
CORNER KICK

- When a player of the defending team plays the ball over the goal line, excluding the portion between the goalposts, the attacking team is awarded a corner kick.

- "The ball is placed inside the corner arc at the nearest corner flagpost." B is clearly inside the arc. A is acceptable because it overlaps the corner arc line.

Ball Position in Corner Area

37

Q Can the kicker move the corner flagpost?

A The corner area provides ample room for a player to take a corner kick. The flagpost must not be moved.

LAW 17
CORNER KICK

Q Which positions may attackers and defenders take in relation to the ball at a corner kick?

A Attackers may be as near to the ball as they wish, but defenders must be at least 10 yards away.

Q If the ball is kicked against a goalpost and returns to the kicker, may he then play it again?

A The kicker may not play the ball a second time until it has been touched by another player. An indirect free kick is awarded from where the ball was played for the second time by the kicker.

CORNER KICK

Q If the ball goes directly into goal from a corner kick would a goal be allowed?

A Yes.

39

Q If the ball swerves over the goal line but back into play, should the game continue?

A The moment the whole of the ball has crossed the goal line it is out of play. The game would be stopped and a goal kick awarded to the defending team.

OFFSIDE

SIMPLY EXPLAINED AND ILLUSTRATED

OFFSIDE

Soccer is a team game. The objective is to combine the skills of the players to move the ball through the opposing team's goal.

The principle of offside is important to this objective because it discourages any player from trying to gain an unfair advantage by being in advance of the ball, near to the goal, to score with the minimum effort.

Other team games, such as rugby, hockey, and water polo, have an offside rule on the same principle—that a player caught in front of the ball is considered out of play, off-the-side, offside. The player must not try to interfere or influence the play in any way.

The offside rule demands alertness and intelligence from all players to assess tactical movements and devise counter measures.

The offside rule contributes much to the attractive fluidity of a soccer game and to the pleasure of those who play or watch.

LAW 11
OFFSIDE

● This law is designed to discourage uninteresting play by attacking players. The game could be played without Law 11, but it could lead to players standing close to goal waiting for the ball for short range attempts at scoring. Such play would require little skill or ability.

● It is not a difficult law to understand if two basic points are clearly established. They are:

(a) A matter of FACT based on the actual position of the player **at the moment the ball is played** by one of his own side;

(b) A matter of OPINION judged by his influence on the play and his motive for being in that position.

FACT

A player is in an **offside position** when he:"is nearer to his opponents' goal line than both the ball and the second-to-last opponent."

OFFSIDE EXAMPLES

When No. 10 passes the ball forward No. 8 is in an OFFSIDE POSITION (having only one opponent between himself and the goal line). He is clearly involved in active play and is adjudged OFFSIDE.

44

LAW 11
OFFSIDE

The ball is thrown in and immediately played back to the thrower, who is now **OFFSIDE**, being in front of the ball and having only one opponent between himself and the goal line.

When No. 7 passes the ball No. 9 is at position A. He moves back to receive the ball at position B. He is adjudged **OFFSIDE** because he was in an **OFFSIDE POSITION** when the ball was played by No. 7 **(FACT)** and is clearly gaining an advantage by being in that position **(OPINION)**.

Note

When the ball is played by a teammate a player cannot put himself on-side by moving back from an **offside position**.

LAW 11
OFFSIDE

No. 6 kicks the ball towards the goal but it is deflected by an opponent to No. 9, who scores. The goal is not allowed because No. 9 was in an **OFFSIDE POSITION** and involved in active play at the moment the ball was kicked by No. 6. The deflection by the opponent in this case does not affect the basic principles of **OFFSIDE**.

No. 8 shoots for goal. The ball rebounds from the crossbar to No. 11 who puts it into the goal. The goal is not valid because although No. 11 was behind the ball when it hit the crossbar, he was in an **OFFSIDE POSITION** (having only one opponent nearer to the goal line) and gained an advantage from that position.

LAW 11
NOT OFFSIDE

At the moment the ball is played towards No. 11 he is not in an offside position because he is level, or in line, with the two last opponents.

A player cannot be offside within his own half of the field of play. In this case the attacker has run forward into the opponents' half after the ball was played.

ATTACKER

BALL

LAW 11
NOT OFFSIDE

No. 9 is not offside because he was not in front of the ball when it was last played by a teammate.

No. 7 is in an offside position when No. 10 kicks the ball into goal. The goal is valid because No. 7 was not involved in active play.

LAW 11
NOT OFFSIDE

No. 7 has moved on to the ball from a forward pass. He was not in front of the ball when kicked by his teammate and is therefore not offside.

A player cannot be offside if he receives the ball direct from a corner kick, a goal kick, or a throw-in

LAW 11
NOT OFFSIDE

A player cannot be offside if he receives the ball from a throw-in. The goal is allowed.

● Summarizing the Offside Law: In every possible situation only two questions need answering:
(i) Is the player in an **offside position** when the ball is played by one of his own side? (This is a matter of FACT.)

If the answer is "Yes" then,
(ii) Is he interfering with play or an opponent, or gaining an advantage? (This is a matter of OPINION.)

SECTION 4

FOULS & MISCONDUCT

WHAT NOT TO DO—
OFFENSES AND PUNISHMENTS

FOULS & MISCONDUCT

At first sight Law 12—Fouls and Misconduct—makes for gloomy reading because it is concerned solely with punishing players. However, on reflection, it is at the heart of the game.

The three basic principles of the spirit of the game are clearly exposed in this law:

Equal opportunity for all players to demonstrate their skills is provided by severely restricting the degree of physical challenges for possession of the ball. To play fairly requires players to avoid challenges which are careless, reckless, or involve excessive force.

Safety is evident in protecting players from dangerous play.

Enjoyment is achieved by defining actions which are unacceptable in a healthy, fair, and exciting sport.

Law 12 comprises three parts:

(i) Major Offenses—direct free kick award

(ii) Other Offenses—indirect free kick award

(iii) Misconduct Offenses—Caution or Dismissal

LAW 12
FOULS & MISCONDUCT

(i) MAJOR OFFENSES

● Ten offenses are penalized by the award of a direct free kick to the opposing team. Nine relate to physical acts against opponents, the tenth being illegally handling the ball.

● A penalty kick is awarded if a player commits any of these offenses inside his own penalty area.

54

EXAMPLES OF MAJOR OFFENSES

Tripping using the legs

Kicking an opponent

LAW 12
FOULS & MISCONDUCT

Tripping by stooping in front of (or behind) an opponent

Jumping at an opponent (The offending player clearly has no intention of playing the ball.)

Charging in a violent or dangerous manner

LAW 12
FOULS & MISCONDUCT

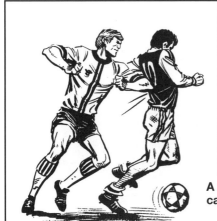

A charge in the back can cause serious injury.

56

Attempting to strike an opponent will be punished as if contact is made.

A goalkeeper who intentionally throws the ball at an opponent is guilty of striking.

FOULS & MISCONDUCT

Holding with the hand or arm

Pulling an opponent's shirt is a holding offense.

Pushing an opponent

LAW 12

FOULS & MISCONDUCT

- Offense: Deliberate handling of the ball with any part of the hand or arm.

- Exception: Does not apply to the goalkeeper handling the ball within his own penalty area.

- Offense: A foul tackle from behind, contact made with opponent before touching the ball. May be a cautionable or dismissal offense depending on the severity of contact.

- Offense: Kicking an opponent. This illustrates a "foot over" tackle, often interpreted as "serious foul play" requiring dismissal of the offending player.

LAW 12
FOULS & MISCONDUCT

● Fair charge

When trying to obtain possession of the ball, it is fair to
attempt to put an opponent
off balance without using
excessive force. Here is an
example of a fair charge,
shoulder to shoulder, arms and
elbows close to the body, ball
within playing distance.

● Unintentional handling

An example of unintentional
handling where the ball is
kicked onto the hand. This is
not an offense.

LAW 12
FOULS & MISCONDUCT

(ii) OTHER OFFENSES

- Eight offenses are penalized by the award of an **indirect free kick** to the opposing team. Five of these are directed to the goalkeeper with the main intention to release the ball into play with minimum delay.

- The first three offenses are:

  (a) playing in a dangerous manner

  (b) impeding the progress of an opponent

  (c) preventing the goalkeeper from releasing the ball from his hands

EXAMPLES OF OTHER OFFENSES

(a) playing in a dangerous manner

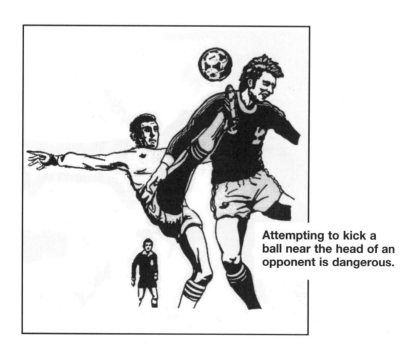

Attempting to kick a ball near the head of an opponent is dangerous.

^LAW 12

FOULS & MISCONDUCT

An overhead "bicycle" kick or a "scissor" kick (shown here) may
be interpreted as dangerous play if attempted near other players.

(b) impeding the progress of an opponent

- Opponents are entitled to make a fair challenge for possession of the ball. When not playing the ball it is an offense to impede (obstruct/block) an opponent by running between the opponent and the ball or interposing the body to block a challenge.

Even though the charge may be fair the ball is not within playing distance and the opponent is impeded from getting to it.

LAW 12

FOULS & MISCONDUCT

Running between an opponent and the ball is an
example of impeding, or obstructing.

This example of "screening" the
ball from an opponent is not
"impeding" because the ball is
being played.

Obstruction is penalized when a player blocks
the opponent's path to the ball when it is not
within playing distance.

FOULS & MISCONDUCT

(c) preventing the goalkeeper
from releasing the ball
from his hands

**The goalkeeper is encouraged to
release the ball from his hands and
into play as soon as possible. It is
an offense to prevent this by block-
ing his path.**

GOALKEEPERS: RESTRICTIONS ON POSSESSION OF THE BALL

● The role of the goalkeeper is to prevent the ball from passing
through the goal. For this purpose the goalkeeper has the special
privilege of touching the ball with the hands inside the penalty
area. To discourage abuses, and with the object of making the
ball available to the other players with the minimum of delay,
Law 12 lists five offenses specifically addressed to goalkeepers.
They relate to excessive possession of the ball and restrictions
on using the hands.

● Use of the hands is not permitted from a direct pass or from a
throw-in from a teammate. To avoid the risk of being penalized
for wasting time, goalkeepers are advised to release the ball within five or six seconds.

LAW 12
FOULS & MISCONDUCT

Possession by goalkeeper

64

● The goalkeeper is allowed no more than four steps when controlling the ball with the hands before releasing it. After releasing the ball the goalkeeper is not allowed to touch it again with his hands until it has been played by another player. He may, however, play the ball with his feet.

● Goalkeepers are not permitted to touch the ball with the hands from a throw-in taken by a teammate. An indirect free kick is awarded where the offense occurred.

Q A goalkeeper falls on the ball and makes no attempt to release it until an opponent has retreated. Is this in order?

A No. The ball must be released within a reasonable time, usually five or six seconds.

LAW 12
FOULS & MISCONDUCT

(iii) MISCONDUCT OFFENSES

- Any player who disregards the principles of the Laws of the Game, by acts of discourtesy towards officials, persistence in committing offenses, or conduct that offends the accepted code of fair play in sport, receives an official Caution from the Referee. This is a warning not to repeat unsporting behavior.

- For offenses of serious foul play, violent conduct, offensive, insulting, or abusive language, or repeated misconduct after receiving a Caution, players are dismissed from a match. Other offenses in this category include spitting at an opponent or any other person and denying an obvious goal-scoring opportunity to an opponent.

- Misconduct of any kind requiring the above sanctions is reported to the appropriate authority (competition, regional, or national association, etc.). Further disciplinary procedures may follow involving periods of suspension from playing and, in some cases, payment of fines.

- The following examples illustrate some acts of misconduct which damage not only the individual reputations of the players concerned but also offend the true ideals of fair play.

65

Showing dissent, by word or action, from any decision given by the Referee. Caution for first offense.

LAW 12
FOULS & MISCONDUCT

**Distracting or attempting to distract an opponent by shouting.
Caution for unsporting behavior.
Indirect kick to the opposing team.**

**Kicking the ball away from the place where the Referee indicates a free
kick is to be taken, showing dissent from the decision, or delaying the
restart of play. (Caution)**

66

FOULS & MISCONDUCT

Foul play during a stoppage in the game. (Dismissal)

An attacking player moves towards the goal with a clear chance to score but is tripped by a defender. In addition to awarding a penalty kick (the offense occurs inside the penalty area), the Referee dismisses the defender for denying an opponent an obvious goal-scoring opportunity. (Law 12—Sending-off offenses, No. 5)

LAW 12
FOULS & MISCONDUCT

68 Misconduct to the Referee at any time, even if it occurs off the field of play, is dealt with as if it occurred during the game.

**Misconduct towards an Assistant Referee (or Fourth Official)
at any time before, during, or after a match. Caution or Dismissal
according to the offense.**

SECTION 5

PLAY TO THE WHISTLE

WHAT MATCH OFFICIALS DO

PLAY TO THE WHISTLE

Match officials are not necessary in games played purely for fun, when the players control their own code of conduct and agree what is fair and unfair, just for the pleasure of kicking a ball among friends.

For organized matches, either as friendly games or in competitions, in which the teams agree to play to the *Laws of the Game*, it is necessary to have a neutral person to decide points of contention and guide the conduct of the match within the rules.

Fully qualified *Referees* and *Assistant Referees* are trained experts in the interpretation and application of the laws.

The *Referee* is delegated many duties and responsibilities by match organizers. Effectively, the Referee is a superintendent appointed to manage, direct, and control a soccer match. Any issue which directly touches on the conduct of a match must be the concern of the *Referee* whether it occurs before, during, or after the event.

71

Section 5 outlines some of the tasks of the *Referee* and, when available, the *Assistant Referees*. It also includes a description of the method of match control employed by the officials—*The Diagonal System*.

Summarizing, an organized soccer match cannot be played to its full potential without the supervision of neutral officials. They apply the principles of the *Spirit of the Game*, ensuring that each player has an *equal opportunity* to demonstrate skills with concern for *safety* within the rules to aim for maximum *enjoyment*.

In soccer, the decisions of the *Referee*, when relating to facts connected with play, are *final* even when they may be seen to be in error. The best advice for any player in doubt is to *Play to the Whistle*.

LAW 5
THE REFEREE

Pencil
Notebook

In Pocket:
Coin
Stopwatch
Extra Whistle
Extra Pencil
CARDS (Red and Yellow)

Wristwatch

Whistle
Attached to
Wrist

**The Referee
Usual Dress and Equipment**

THE REFEREE

● The Referee has the power to penalize when play has been stopped.

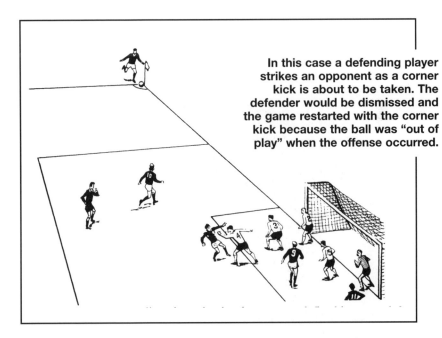

In this case a defending player strikes an opponent as a corner kick is about to be taken. The defender would be dismissed and the game restarted with the corner kick because the ball was "out of play" when the offense occurred.

73

The attacking player (No. 8) is fouled but the Referee has the power to refrain from stopping the play if it would be to the advantage of the offended team to continue. However, if the advantage is not realized within a few seconds the Referee can penalize the original offense.

LAW 5
THE REFEREE

A defending player attempts to prevent a goal being scored by deliberately handling the ball. If the ball enters goal the Referee will allow the goal and not award a penalty kick for the handling offense. If the ball does not enter the goal the offending player is dismissed for denying opponents an obvious goal opportunity.

- The Referee has the power to stop the game if, in his opinion, a player is seriously injured.

- Any player bleeding from an injury must leave the field and will only be allowed to return when the bleeding has been stopped.

THE REFEREE

● No person, other than the players and Assistant Referees, may enter the field of play without the Referee's permission.

In the situation shown here the team official may be warned and reported.

● To communicate the severity of a disciplinary sanction to the player concerned and to others, the Referee produces a card:

Yellow card = Caution
Red card = Dismissal from the match

LAW 5
THE REFEREE

SIGNALS—BY THE REFEREE

BY LAW
Only two signals are mandatory in the Laws of the Game:

- Indirect Free Kick—one arm raised above the head (c)

- Discipline Cards—display of a colored card to an offending player

APPROVED SIGNALS
Instruction to players:

- Play on Advantage—the Referee observes an offense but decides to apply the advantage option and signals play to continue (a)

- Direct Free Kick—a hand and arm signal to indicate direction of free kick (b)

- Penalty Kick—pointing to the penalty mark (d)

- Other Approved Signals— pointing to the appropriate position for a throw-in, goal kick, corner kick, free kick

INFORMATIVE (UNOFFICIAL)

- Instinctive gestures communicating the nature of offenses, for example, handling the ball, pushing, etc. (e) (f)

(a) Play on Advantage

(b) Direct Free Kick (direction)

(c) Indirect Free Kick

(d) Penalty Kick

(e) Handling the Ball

(f) Pushing

LAW 6
ASSISTANT REFEREES

- Neutral Assistant Referees, when appointed, are selected from a panel of qualified referees. As their title suggests, they assist the Referee to control a match in accordance with his instructions and the Laws of the Game.

Here, an Assistant Referee reports an offense by an attacking player which he noticed immediately prior to the scoring of a goal. The Referee, if he has not observed the incident, may act on the advice and cancel the goal.

If the ball strikes an Assistant Referee and is deflected over a boundary line the game is restarted with a throw-in, goal kick, or corner kick. In this case it would be a corner kick because a defending player last touched the ball and it was deflected over the goal line.

LAW 6
ASSISTANT REFEREES

SIGNALS FOR THE INFORMATION OF THE REFEREE

● Flag signals indicate to the Referee when the ball goes out of play over a touch- or goal line and the correct decision, for example, goal kick, corner kick, or which side is entitled to a throw-in.

A special signal draws the Referee's attention to a request for substitution.

Substitution

Corner Kick

Throw-in Direction

Goal Kick

⌐AW 6
ASSISTANT REFEREES

SIGNALS—OFFSIDE

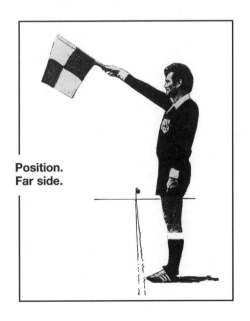

Offside: A series of signals to indicate when a player, in an offside position, may be penalized and the position of the offense.

Position. Center of field.

Offside. Flag in vertical position.

Position. Far side.

Position. Near side.

MATCH OFFICIALS

THE DIAGONAL SYSTEM

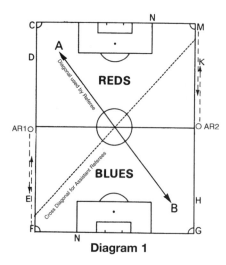

Diagram 1

- The imaginary diagonal used by the Referee is the line A-B.

- The opposite diagonal, used by the Assistant Referees AR1 and AR2, is adjusted to the position of the Referee.

- If the Referee is near A, AR2 will be at a point between M and K. When the Referee is at B, AR1 will be between E and F. This gives two officials control of the respective "danger zones," one at each side of the field.

- AR1 adopts the Reds as his side; AR2 adopts the Blues. As Red forwards move toward the Blue goal, AR1 keeps in line with the second-to-last defender so, in actual practice, he will rarely get into the Reds' half of the field. Similarly, AR2 keeps in line with the second-to-last Red defender and will rarely get into the Blues' half.

- At corner kicks or penalty kicks, the Assistant in the half where the corner kick or penalty kick occurs positions himself at N, M, or F, according to the Referee's instructions. The Referee then takes position.

- The Diagonal System fails if AR2 gets between G and H when the Referee is at B, or when AR1 is near C or D when the Referee is at A, because there are two officials in the same place. This should be avoided.

Note

Some Referees prefer to use the opposite diagonal, from F to M, in which case the Assistants adjust their patrol accordingly.

MATCH OFFICIALS

THE DIAGONAL SYSTEM

Development of attack

- Ball moves out to left wing. Referee (R) slightly off diagonal to be near play.

- Assistant Referee AR2 level with second last defender.

- Two officials, therefore, up with play.

- AR1 in position for clearances and possible counterattack.

**Free kick near goal
(just outside penalty area)**

- Players ● and ○ line up for free kick.

- Referee (R) takes up his position just off his diagonal so that he is placed accurately to judge offside. AR2 is more advanced but can watch for offside and fouls and also is in a good position to act as goal judge in the event of a direct shot being taken.

SECTION 6

SOCCER GUIDELINES

GUIDELINES FOR
THE SOCCER FAMILY

THE FIFA FAIR PLAY CAMPAIGN

CODE OF CONDUCT—10 GOLDEN RULES

1 play to win

2 play fair

3 observe the Laws of the Game

4 respect opponents, teammates, referees, officials, and spectators

5 accept defeat with dignity

6 promote the interests of soccer

7 reject corruption, drugs, racism, violence, and other dangers to our sport

8 help others resist corrupting pressures

9 denounce those who attempt to discredit our sport

10 honor those who defend soccer's good reputation

85

"For the Good of the Game"

PLAYER

You want to have fun and improve your game. Knowing something about the rules will add to your interest in soccer and help avoid problems on the field.

EQUIPMENT

Before every game check your equipment for any item which may prove to be dangerous to yourself or your opponents. Footwear, in particular the studs you choose to suit the field surface condition, needs special care. The Referee may ask you to remove items of jewelry.

STARTING PLAY

Remember the ball is not in play until kicked. The signal for the kick is not the signal for you to move nearer than 10 yards to the ball.

BALL OUT OF PLAY

The *whole* of the ball must be over the boundary lines before it is out of play.

FREE KICK POSITION

Free kicks must be taken from the place where the offense occurred with the ball stationary.

10 YARDS, PLEASE

Check what 10 yards means—for example, the center circle has a 10-yard radius—and be at least this far away as soon as a free kick is awarded against your team. You will avoid a yellow card.

OFFSIDE

It's very important to understand this rule because your team loses a chance to score and the ball is given to the opposing team every time you are caught offside.

Study carefully the explanations and illustrations in Section 3. In particular realize that **Offside** is first a matter of **Fact**, i.e. **your position** in relation to the ball and opposing players, and second a matter

PLAYER

of **the Opinion of the Referee** as to your involvement in **active play**, and any advantage you may gain by being in an **offside position**.

Offside position is judged at the **moment the ball touches or is played by a teammate, not where you are when you receive the ball**.

(a) You cannot be offside if you are **behind the ball**. If you are ahead of the ball be aware of the positions of the opponents. Try to keep at least two players between you and their goal line.

(b) If you are in an **offside position**, get back behind the ball or avoid the next **area of active play** to convince the Referee that you are not influencing play or trying to gain an advantage.

(c) You cannot be offside if you receive the ball direct from **a goal kick, a corner kick, or a throw-in**.

87

UNFAIR PLAY
You want to show your skills with the ball. So do opponents. Challenges for possession often involve hard physical contact. You will avoid being penalized if you control your challenges with care by not being reckless or using excessive force.

CHARGING AN OPPONENT
You may charge an opponent fairly but not when the ball is not within playing distance or when you are making no attempt to play it.

SPORTING BEHAVIOR
Nobody enjoys the spectacle of a player being cautioned or sent off. Understand from Law 12 what actions are unacceptable and can be avoided.

PENALTY KICKS
The important points to remember are:

(a) the positions of the players

(b) players must remain at the proper distances until the ball is in play

(c) the ball is in play when it has been kicked forward

PLAYER

THROW-IN POSITION

Throw-ins must be taken from the point where the ball crossed the touchline.

GOALKEEPERS

You must know the following:

(a) Wear colors which distinguish you from other players and the Referee.

(b) The rules are strict about the amount of time that you are allowed possession of the ball and when you must not touch it with your hands.

(c) When you take the ball into your hands you must release it into play without taking more than four steps or more than a few seconds. If you exceed about six seconds you risk giving the opponents a free kick in a very dangerous position.

(d) Avoid any tactics which may be interpreted as wasting time.

(e) When challenged for the ball, avoid distracting opponents by shouting.

(f) You are not allowed to pull down the crossbar to prevent the ball from entering the goal. You will be cautioned.

(g) You will be penalized if you touch the ball with your hands if a teammate deliberately kicks it to you or throws it direct to you from a throw-in.

(h) Regarding item (c), understand that if you deliberately parry the ball with your hands you are still considered to be in possession. Release the ball without touching it again with your hands.

(i) When facing a penalty kick you may move **along** your goal line before the ball is kicked, but not **from** it—for example, advancing towards the ball. Also avoid any gestures which may be interpreted as attempts to distract the penalty kicker. This is **unsporting behavior**.

(j) If you intend to change places with a teammate, be sure to advise the Referee in advance.

REFEREE

You play a vital role in the amount of pleasure people obtain from soccer.

Every game poses a variety of problems requiring instant and correct decisions. Only by clearly understanding the purpose and application of each Law can you carry out your duties efficiently. Some problems will arise which do not have written answers. These must be solved with the application of common sense. Your feeling for what is fair and unfair will guide you to the right decision.

For qualified Referees, the following guidelines are intended as reminders of the basic duties and responsibilities you have been trained to accept.

For other members of the soccer family, a glance at the guidelines will give insight into the contribution of match officials to keep soccer a clean, healthy, and enjoyable family sport.

89

REFEREE

Section 1   COMPONENTS

CHECKLIST Establish a routine method of checking all components by making a list of items to be examined. Your list should include the following:

(a) **FIELD**—condition of the playing surface, line markings, dimensions, inside areas, penalty and center marks.

(b) **GOALS**—safety of construction, anchorage, size, color, nets.

(c) **FLAGPOSTS**—positions, height, safety of construction.

(d) **BALL**—shape, size, pressure to suit game conditions, conformity with FIFA standards where necessary. Spare ball(s).

(e) **PLAYERS**—number on each team, substitutes, names, goalkeepers.

(f) **PLAYERS' EQUIPMENT**—colors, footwear, dangerous ornaments.

(g) **TIME**—complete checks to allow sufficient time to adjust incorrect items.

Section 2   RULES OF PLAY

COMPETITION RULES Check for any additions to or variations from the Laws which have been agreed to between the competing teams. In particular:

(a) **COMPONENTS**—for players under 16 years of age, women, and veteran players.

(b) **TIMING**—for players in item (a), periods of extra time. Allow for the time lost due to delays for substitutions, injuries, time-wasting tactics, and any other cause at your discretion. Players have a right to an interval at halftime not exceeding 15 minutes.

REFEREE

(c) **FREE KICKS**—Allow free kicks to be taken as quickly as possible so that the offending team does not gain an advantage by using delay to organize their defense.

    (i)   The ball must be stationary before kick is taken.

    (ii) Caution any player attempting to delay a free kick, for example, by moving the ball from its correct position.

    (iii) Caution any player of the offending team who refuses to retire to the proper distance before the kick is taken.

    (iv) At an indirect free kick raise one arm before the signal to take the kick.

(d) **GOALS**—Do not award a goal unless you are sure that the ball has wholly crossed the goal line between the posts and under the crossbar.

    (i)   Check with your Assistant Referees before awarding a goal. A goal cannot be cancelled after play has been restarted.

    (ii) Keep a record of each goal as it is scored.

Section 3   OFFSIDE

BASICS You have to first decide if the player is in an **offside position**. This is not an offense until you make a second decision based on your judgement of the player's influence on the play.

(a) **OFFSIDE POSITION**—Is the player in front of the ball in the opponents' half? If so, and if he is nearer to the goal line than the second-to-last opponent, the player is in an **offside position**.

(b) **OFFSIDE OFFENSE**—Is the player involved in the zone of play, for example, by moving towards an opponent or the ball or gaining an advantage? If so, this is an **offside offense.**

(c) **MOMENT OF ASSESSMENT**—Offside decisions are assessed at the moment the ball touches or is played by a teammate.

REFEREE

Section 4   FOULS—MISCONDUCT

FOUL PLAY—Most foul play occurs when two players challenge for possession of the ball. Physical contact is inevitable in most instances and is an accepted part of the game. However, challenges must be kept under control, and to be fair, they must not be careless, reckless, or involve excessive force.

DANGEROUS PLAY—Attempting to play the ball may sometimes put an opponent in danger, for example, when the ball is close to the opponent's head or chest. An indirect free kick is the correct award.

YOUNG AND WOMEN PLAYERS—It is advisable to take special care, in matches with young or women players, to interpret physical challenges on the side of caution in order to reduce the risk of injuries.

MISCONDUCT—A policy of strict control over all forms of misconduct is recommended, not only to guide the particular match in your charge, but also to protect the overall image of the game. In particular:

(a) **UNSPORTING BEHAVIOR**—Attempts to gain an unfair advantage, contesting decisions, and disregard for the Laws of the Game form the general character of unsporting behavior in soccer. The purpose of cautioning players for any act under this heading is to reduce the need for more serious disciplinary action in subsequent play.

(b) **SERIOUS MISCONDUCT**—Any player who continues to behave in an unsporting manner after receiving a caution, who commits serious foul play, who behaves violently, who insults opponents or officials, or denies the opposing team a fair chance to score a goal, deserves the penalty of dismissal from a match and further punishment by the competent authorities.

(c) **PREVENTION**—A timely word of advice to players who appear to be losing self-control will help to complete the match without the necessity for severe disciplinary action.

REFEREE

Section 5 PLAY TO THE WHISTLE

MATCH CONTROL—You may or may not have the aid of Assistant Referees to control your match. Whatever the situation give careful thought to pregame conditions and how they may affect your method of control. You can form your opinion during the pregame check of the components listed in Section 1.

(a) **ADVANTAGE**—You have a few seconds of reflection to decide if a decision to allow advantage will have the desired effect. Do not hesitate to call back the play if it does not work. Also, do not allow an offender to escape a caution or dismissal (where appropriate) if it does work.

(b) **INJURED PLAYERS**—Stop the game immediately if a player appears to be seriously injured. You may save the player from long-term handicap, or worse. Do not wait for the players to kick the ball out of play—it is your duty to act quickly, particularly when a player has a head injury.

93

(c) **MEDICAL ASSISTANCE**—Find out before the game where you can call for aid should it be needed promptly.

(d) **SLIGHT INJURIES**—Wait for a normal stoppage to allow slightly injured players to leave the field for treatment. Where young or women players are involved it is advisable to err on the side of discretion and stop play if in doubt.

(e) **SIMULATED INJURIES**—Be alert to players who pretend to be injured to gain an advantage—for example, delay—or to have an opponent disciplined.

COACHING—A coach is allowed to issue instructions to players during a match provided that it is done in a responsible manner. The person delegated to coach should be identified to you before the start of play.

(a) **TECHNICAL AREA**—Check whether such an area exists at your match. If not, find out from the coaches where they will be located.

(b) **CONDUCT**—Be aware of any abuse of the coaching privilege and report any unsporting behavior to the competent authority.

REFEREE

ILLEGAL ENTRY INTO THE FIELD—Do not allow officials or any other person into the field of play without your permission.

SIGNALS—The Laws do not specify any code of signals apart from the raising of one arm to signify an indirect free kick. However, simple and discreet gestures, for example, touching a hand to indicate handball, will help you communicate with players and others and possibly reduce dissent.

ASSISTANT REFEREES

Neutral Officials—You are a fully qualified Referee appointed to a match as an Assistant Referee. Previous to 1996 your title was Linesman. The new status recognized the importance of your task to assist the match Referee in coping with increasing responsibilities. Apart from your basic duties, listed in Law 6, the following guidelines will add to the effectiveness of your cooperation with the Referee. All are subject to instructions you receive from the Referee.

94

COMPONENTS
Walk the field to check with the Referee. Bring to the Referee's attention any incorrect items.

SUBSTITUTES
Assist with the checking of names, where they are located, and any special competition rules to be observed.

TIMING OF PLAY
Time the play as if you are the Referee. Does the Referee need a signal to indicate time remaining?

OFF-THE-BALL INCIDENTS
Any incidents of serious foul play, violent conduct, or any other misconduct which the Referee has not yet observed must be notified without delay.

ASSISTANT REFEREES

OFFSIDE
Know what the Referee wants in monitoring the play for offside situations, particularly at free kicks near the penalty area. Use field markings as references to judge zones of active play.

COACHING
Draw the Referee's attention to any misconduct or movement outside of the technical area.

IDENTIFICATION OF OFFENDERS
Make a note of players disciplined for misconduct to ensure correct identification in match reports.

THIRD TEAM
The Referee and the two Assistant Referees form the "third team" at a match. The degree of cooperation you achieve will have an important bearing on the efficiency of control and the enjoyment of play.

95

CLUB ASSISTANTS

Fully qualified neutral Assistant Referees may not be available. The two teams in a match are required, sometimes as a mandatory competition rule, to provide a person to act as a Club Assistant to the Referee.

DUTIES
Both Club Assistants must report to the Referee before the start of the match for instructions as to the manner in which they can cooperate in the conduct of the match.

GENERAL
The Referee usually asks for a signal to indicate that the ball has passed out of play over the touchline and which side is entitled to the throw-in. Other forms of assistance may be delegated, subject always to the fact that the Referee's decision is final.

COACH

Your role in soccer was recognized in 1993 when the International Football Association Board agreed that you may convey tactical instructions to your players during the course of a match. This was an historical concession intended to "add to the quality of play."

It was granted on two main conditions:
(a) that you give your instructions from a specific location, a technical area when this can be provided, and;
(b) that you behave in a responsible manner.

Because it is required that only one person is allowed to issue instructions it is necessary that you identify yourself to the Referee before the start of the match.

After giving instructions you are required to return to your position.

If a formally marked technical area is not provided advise the Referee of the specific location from where you wish to give your instructions. You should remain in this location.

You are usually a person of much experience in soccer and have in your charge young players whose characters are forming at an impressionable age. Apart from the technical guidance you are qualified to impart in the playing of the game, you are a strong influence on the degree of respect your players show for fair play and their attitudes towards opponents, match officials, and spectators.

During a match you are as emotionally involved as the players because you want to obtain a good result. However, in granting the concession of coaching during the play, the International Football Association Board expects you to accept the same criteria for correct behavior as is required of your players.

ORGANIZERS

You may be a team manager, club official, competition organizer, or a volunteer giving your time so that others may share your affection for soccer.

For the correct organization of each match the club has several duties and responsibilities. The following notes outline the main points.

COMPETITIONS—Clubs accept to comply with the rules of competitions, which may vary in some respects with the Laws of the Game, for example, in the number of substitutes, periods of play, extra time, etc. It is the duty of the club to know both the Laws and agreed variations.

MATCH OFFICIALS—The club in charge of match arrangements is responsible for the welfare of the match officials before, during, and after the match.

CLUB DISCIPLINE—Each club is responsible for the proper conduct of its players and officials.

MATCH ARRANGEMENTS—The club in charge is responsible for providing:
(a) a field of play, correctly marked in accordance with Law 1, together with proper goals and corner posts with flags. Goal nets are desirable but not compulsory.
(b) the match ball plus spare balls if possible.
(c) suitable dressing and washing facilities for the players and match officials.
(d) whenever possible, a suitable barrier between the playing field and spectators. Sufficient space should be allowed to avoid interference with play and the patrol of Assistant Referees.
(e) the match officials with full details of match location, time of kickoff, and any other relevant information.

CONSULTATION—Consult with the Referee on any matter which may affect the correct conduct of a match, for example, security when many spectators are expected.

97

SUPPORTERS

You probably support a particular club and enjoy the soccer family atmosphere as you marvel at the skills of your favorite players. Your presence and encouragement stimulates players to play well.

You can help people continue to enjoy soccer in other ways. Here are some suggestions:

FAIR PLAY—Insist on fair play, not only from players of other teams but also from your own favorites.

MATCH OFFICIALS—Appreciate the task of the officials from the guidelines in this publication. They try to ensure that each match is played to the spirit as well as to the letter of the rules. They are members of the soccer family and deserve your support.

PLAYERS' SKILLS—Exciting skills are part of the joy of soccer, whether shown by your own players or opponents. Applaud both.

COMBAT NEGATIVE INFLUENCES—The FIFA Campaign for Fair Play appeals to the whole soccer family to recognize and combat dangers to soccer. Support FIFA by denouncing anyone who discredits our sport by corruption, drugs, racism, or violence.

OTHER SUPPORTERS—Those who support opposing teams share your passion for the game. They, too, are members of the soccer family. Respect and salute them.

TO ALL SUPPORTERS! HELP KEEP SOCCER A CLEAN, HEALTHY, AND EXCITING SPORT, DESERVING OF THE TITLE:

"THE PEOPLE'S GAME"

THE OFFICIAL LAWS

SEVENTEEN LAWS PLUS DECISIONS OF THE INTERNATIONAL FOOTBALL ASSOCIATION BOARD

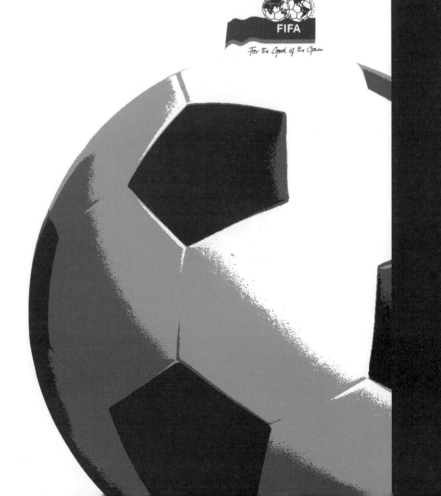

FIFA

For the Good of the Game

THE OFFICIAL LAWS

NOTES ON THE LAWS OF THE GAME

MODIFICATIONS

Subject to the agreement of the national association concerned and provided the principles of these Laws are maintained, the Laws may be modified in their application to matches for players of under 16 years of age, for women soccer players, and for veteran soccer players (over 35 years of age).

ANY OR ALL OF THE FOLLOWING MODIFICATIONS ARE PERMISSIBLE:

● size of the field of play

● size, weight, and material of the ball

● width between the goalposts and height of the crossbar from the ground

● the duration of the periods of play

● substitutions

Further modifications are only allowed with the consent of the International Football Association Board.

MALE AND FEMALE

References to the male gender in the Laws of the Game in respect of referees, assistant referees, players, and officials are for simplification and apply to both males and females.

KEY

Throughout the Laws of the Game the following symbol is used:

* Unless covered by the Special Circumstances listed in Law 8— The Start and Restart of Play

LAW 1—THE FIELD OF PLAY*   *See page 4

DIMENSIONS

The field of play must be rectangular. The length of the touchline must be greater than the length of the goal line.

Length: minimum 100 yd. (90 m.)
                  maximum 130 yd. (120 m.)

Width: minimum 50 yd. (45 m.)
                  maximum 100 yd. (90m.)

INTERNATIONAL MATCHES

Length: minimum 110 yd. (100 m.)
                  maximum 120 yd. (110 m.)

Width: minimum 70 yd. (64 m.)
                  maximum 80 yd. (75 m.)

FIELD MARKINGS

The field of play is marked with lines. These lines belong to the areas of which they are boundaries.

The two longer boundary lines are called touchlines. The two shorter lines are called goal lines.

All lines are not more than 5 in. (12 cm.) wide.

The field of play is divided into two halves by a halfway line.

The center mark is indicated at the midpoint of the halfway line. A circle with a radius of 10 yd. (9.15 m.) is marked around it.

THE GOAL AREA

A goal area is defined at each end of the field as follows:

Two lines are drawn at right angles to the goal line, 6 yd. (5.5 m.) from the inside of each goalpost. These lines extend into the field of play for a distance of 6 yd. (5.5 m.) and are joined by a line drawn parallel with the goal line. The area bounded by these lines and the goal line is the goal area.

THE PENALTY AREA

A penalty area is defined at each end of the field as follows:

Two lines are drawn at right angles to the goal line, 18 yd. (16.5 m.) from the inside of each goalpost. These lines extend into the field of play for a distance of 18 yd. (16.5 m.) and are joined by a line drawn parallel with the goal line. The area bounded by these lines and the goal line is the penalty area.

Within each penalty area a penalty mark is made 12 yd. (11 m.) from the midpoint between the goalposts and equidistant to them. An arc of a circle with a radius of 10 yd. (9.15 m.) from each penalty mark is drawn outside the penalty area.

FLAGPOSTS

A flagpost, not less than 5 ft. (1.5 m.) high, with a non-pointed top and a flag, is placed at each corner.

Flagposts may also be placed at each end of the halfway line, not less than 1 yd. (1 m.) outside the touchline.

THE CORNER ARC

A quarter circle with a radius of 1 yd. (1 m.) from each corner flagpost is drawn inside the field of play.

GOALS

Goals must be placed on the center of each goal line.

They consist of two upright posts equidistant from the corner flagposts and joined at the top by a horizontal crossbar.

The distance between the posts is 8 yd. (7.32 m.) and the distance from the lower edge of the crossbar to the ground is 8 ft. (2.44 m.).

Both goalposts and the crossbar have the same width and depth, which do not exceed 5 in. (12 cm.). The goal lines are the same width as that of the goalposts and the crossbar. Nets may be attached to the goals and the ground behind the goal, provided that they are properly supported and do not interfere with the goalkeeper.

The goalposts and crossbars must be white.

SAFETY

Goals must be anchored securely to the ground. Portable goals may only be used if they satisfy this requirement.

DECISIONS OF THE INTERNATIONAL FOOTBALL ASSOCIATION BOARD

● DECISION 1

If the crossbar becomes displaced or broken, play is stopped until it has been repaired or replaced in position. If a repair is not possible, the match is abandoned. The use of rope to replace the crossbar is not permitted. If the crossbar can be repaired, the match is restarted with a dropped ball at the place where the ball was located when play was stopped.*

● DECISION 2

Goalposts and crossbars must be made of wood, metal, or other approved material. Their shape may be square, rectangular, round, or elliptical and they must not be dangerous to players.

● DECISION 3

No kind of commercial advertising, whether real or virtual, is permitted on the field of play and field equipment (including the goal nets and the areas they enclose) from the time the teams enter the field of play until they have left it at halftime and from the time the teams reenter the field of play until the end of the match. In particular, no advertising material of any kind may be displayed on goals, nets, flagposts, or their flags. No extraneous equipment (cameras, microphones, etc.) may be attached to these items.

● DECISION 4

The reproduction, whether real or virtual, of representative logos or emblems of FIFA, confederations, national associations, leagues, clubs, or other bodies, is forbidden on the field of play and field equipment (including the goal nets and the areas they enclose) during playing time, as described in Decision 3.

● DECISION 5

A mark may be made off the field of play, 10 yd. (9.15 m.) from the corner arc and at right angles to the goal lines to ensure that this distance is observed when a corner kick is being taken.

LAW 2—THE BALL

QUALITIES AND MEASUREMENTS

The ball is:

- spherical
- made of leather or other suitable material
- of a circumference of not more than 28 in. (70 cm.) and not less than 27 in. (68 cm.)
- not more than 16 oz. (450 g.) in weight and not less than 14 oz. (410 g.) at the start of the match
- of a pressure equal to 0.6 -1.1 atmosphere (600-1100 g/cm2) at sea level (8.5 lb./sq. in. -15.6 lb./sq. in.)

REPLACEMENT OF A DEFECTIVE BALL

If the ball bursts or becomes defective during the course of a match:

- the match is stopped
- the match is restarted by dropping the replacement ball at the place where the first ball became defective*

If the ball bursts or becomes defective while not in play at a kick-off, goal kick, corner kick, free kick, penalty kick, or throw-in:

- the match is restarted accordingly

The ball may not be changed during the match without the authority of the Referee.

DECISIONS OF THE INTERNATIONAL FOOTBALL ASSOCIATION BOARD

● DECISION 1

In competition matches, only soccer balls which meet the minimum technical requirements stipulated in Law 2 are permitted for use.

In FIFA competition matches, and in competition matches organized under the auspices of the confederations, acceptance of a soccer ball for use is conditional upon the soccer ball bearing one of the following three designations:

 the official "FIFA APPROVED" logo, **or**

 the official "FIFA INSPECTED" logo, **or**

the reference "INTERNATIONAL MATCHBALL STANDARD"

Such a designation on a soccer ball indicates that it has been tested officially and found to be in compliance with specific technical requirements, different for each category and additional to the minimum specifications stipulated in Law 2. The list of additional requirements specific to each of the respective categories must be approved by the International F. A. Board. The institutes conducting the tests are subject to the approval of FIFA.

National association competitions may require the use of balls bearing any one of these three designations.

In all other matches the ball used must satisify the requirements of Law 2.

● DECISION 2

In FIFA competition matches and in competition matches organized under the auspices of the confederations and national associations, no kind of commercial advertising on the ball is permitted, except for the emblem of the competition, the competition organizer, and the authorized trademark of the manufacturer. The competition regulations may restrict the size and number of such markings.

LAW 3—THE NUMBER OF PLAYERS

PLAYERS
A match is played by two teams, each consisting of not more than eleven players, one of whom is the goalkeeper. A match may not start if either team consists of fewer than seven players.

OFFICIAL COMPETITIONS
Up to a maximum of three substitutes may be used in any match played in an official competition organized under the auspices of FIFA, the confederations, or the national associations.

The rules of the competition must state how many substitutes may be nominated, from three up to a maximum of seven.

OTHER MATCHES
In other matches, up to five substitutes may be used, provided that:

- the teams concerned reach agreement on a maximum number
- the Referee is informed before the match

If the Referee is not informed, or if no agreement is reached before the start of the match, no more than three substitutes are allowed.

ALL MATCHES
In all matches the names of the subsitutes must be given to the Referee prior to the start of the match. Substitutes not so named may not take part in the match.

SUBSTITUTION PROCEDURE
To replace a player by a substitute, the following conditions must be observed:

- the Referee is informed before any proposed substitution is made
- a substitute only enters the field of play after the player being replaced has left and after receiving a signal from the Referee
- a substitute only enters the field of play at the halfway line and during a stoppage in the match
- a substitution is completed when a substitute enters the field of play
- from that moment, the substitute becomes a player and the player he has replaced ceases to be a player
- a player who has been replaced takes no further part in the match
- all substitutes are subject to the authority and jurisdiction of the Referee, whether called upon to play or not

CHANGING THE GOALKEEPER

Any of the other players may change places with the goalkeeper, provided that:

- *the Referee is informed before the change is made*
- *the change is made during a stoppage in the match*

INFRINGEMENTS/SANCTIONS

If a substitute enters the field of play without the Referee's permission:

- *play is stopped*
- *the substitute is cautioned, shown the yellow card, and required to leave the field of play*
- *play is restarted with a dropped ball at the place it was located when play was stopped**

If a player changes places with the goalkeeper without the Referee's permission before the change is made:

- *play continues*
- *the players concerned are cautioned and shown the yellow card when the ball is next out of play*

For any other infringements of this Law:

- *the players concerned are cautioned and shown the yellow card*

RESTART OF PLAY

If play is stopped by the Referee to administer a caution:

- *the match is restarted by an indirect free kick, to be taken by a player of the opposing team from the place where the ball was located when play was stopped**

PLAYERS AND SUBSTITUTES SENT OFF

A player who has been sent off before the kickoff may be replaced only by one of the named substitutes.

A named substitute who has been sent off, either before the kickoff or after play has started, may not be replaced.

DECISIONS OF THE INTERNATIONAL FOOTBALL ASSOCIATION BOARD

● DECISION 1

Subject to the overriding conditions of Law 3, the minimum number of players in a team is left to the discretion of national associations. The Board is of the opinion, however, that a match should not continue if there are fewer than seven players in either team.

● DECISION 2

The coach may convey tactical instructions to the players during the match. He and the other officials must remain within the confines of the technical area, where such an area is provided, and they must behave in a responsible manner.

LAW 4—THE PLAYERS' EQUIPMENT

SAFETY

A player must not use equipment or wear anything which is dangerous to himself or another player (including any kind of jewelry.)

BASIC EQUIPMENT

The basic compulsory equipment of a player is:

- *a jersey or shirt*
- *shorts—if thermal undershorts are worn, they are of the same main color as the shorts*
- *stockings*
- *shinguards*
- *footwear*

SHINGUARDS

- *are covered entirely by the stockings*
- *are made of a suitable material (rubber, plastic, or similar substances)*
- *provide a reasonable degree of protection*

GOALKEEPERS

- *each goalkeeper wears colors which distinguish him from the other players, the Referee, and the Assistant Referees*

INFRINGEMENTS/SANCTIONS

For any infringement of this Law:

- *play need not be stopped*
- *the player at fault is instructed by the Referee to leave the field of play to correct his equipment*
- *the player leaves the field of play when the ball next ceases to be in play, unless he has already corrected his equipment*
- *any player required to leave the field of play to correct his equipment does not reenter without the Referee's permission*
- *the Referee checks that the player's equipment is correct before allowing him to reenter the field of play*
- *the player is only allowed to reenter the field of play when the ball is out of play*

A player who has been required to leave the field of play because of an infringement of this Law and who enters (or reenters) the field of play without the Referee's permission is cautioned and shown the yellow card.

RESTART OF PLAY

If play is stopped by the Referee to administer a caution:

- *the match is restarted by an indirect free kick taken by a player of the opposing side, from the place where the ball was located when the Referee stopped the match**

LAW 5—THE REFEREE

THE AUTHORITY OF THE REFEREE

Each match is controlled by a Referee who has full authority to enforce the Laws of the Game in connection with the match to which he has been appointed.

POWERS AND DUTIES

The Referee:

- enforces the Laws of the Game
- controls the match in cooperation with the Assistant Referees and, where applicable, with the fourth official
- ensures that any ball used meets with the requirements of Law 2
- ensures that the players' equipment meets the requirements of Law 4
- acts as timekeeper and keeps a record of the match
- stops, suspends, or terminates the match, at his discretion, for any infringements of the Laws
- stops, suspends, or terminates the match because of outside interference of any kind
- stops the match if, in his opinion, a player is seriously injured and ensures that he is removed from the field of play
- allows play to continue until the ball is out play if a player is, in his opinion, only slightly injured
- ensures that any player bleeding from a wound leaves the field of play. The player may only return on receiving a signal from the Referee, who must be satisfied that the bleeding has stopped
- allows play to continue when the team against which an offense has been committed will benefit from such an advantage and penalizes the original offense if the anticipated advantage does not ensue at that time
- punishes the more serious offense when a player commits more than one offense at the same time
- takes disciplinary action against players guilty of cautionable and sending-off offenses. He is not obliged to take this action immediately but must do so when the ball next goes out of play
- takes action against team officials who fail to conduct themselves in a responsible manner and may at his discretion expel them from the field of play and its immediate surrounds
- acts on the advice of the Assistant Referees regarding incidents which he has not seen
- ensures that no unauthorized persons enter the field of play
- restarts the match after it has been stopped
- provides the appropriate authorities with a match report which includes information on any disciplinary action taken against players, and/or team officials, and any other incidents which occurred before, during, or after the match

DECISIONS OF THE REFEREE

The decisions of the Referee regarding facts connected with play are final.

The Referee may only change a decision on realizing that it is incorrect or, at his discretion, on the advice of an Assistant Referee, provided that he has not restarted play.

DECISIONS OF THE INTERNATIONAL FOOTBALL ASSOCIATION BOARD

● DECISION 1

A Referee (or where applicable, an Assistant Referee or fourth official) is not held liable for:

any kind of injury suffered by a player, official, or spectator

any damage to property of any kind

any other loss suffered by any individual, club, company, association, or other body, which is due, or which may be due, to any decision which he may take under the terms of the Laws of the Game, or in respect of the normal procedures required to hold, play, and control a match.

This may include:

- a decision that the condition of the field of play or its surrounds or that the weather conditions are such as to allow or not to allow a match to take place
- a decision to abandon a match for whatever reason
- a decision as to the condition of the fixtures or equipment used during a match including the goalposts, crossbar, flagposts, and the ball
- a decision to stop or not to stop a match due to spectator interference or any problem in the spectator area
- a decision to stop or not to stop play to allow an injured player to be removed from the field of play for treatment
- a decision to request or insist that an injured player be removed from the field of play for treatment
- a decision to allow or not to allow a player to wear certain apparel or equipment
- a decision (insofar as this may be his responsibility) to allow or not to allow any persons (including team or stadium officials, security officers, photographers, or other media representatives) to be present in the vicinity of the field of play
- any other decision which he may take in accordance with the Laws of the Game or in conformity with his duties under the terms of FIFA, confederation, national association, or league rules or regulations under which the match is played

● DECISION 2

In tournaments or competitions where a fourth official is appointed, his role and duties must be in accordance with the guidelines approved by the International Football Association Board.

● DECISION 3

Facts connected with play shall include whether a goal is scored or not and the result of the match.

112

LAW 6—THE ASSISTANT REFEREES

DUTIES

Two Assistant Referees are appointed whose duties, subject to the decision of the Referee, are to indicate:

- when the whole of the ball has passed out of the field of play
- which side is entitled to a corner kick, goal kick, or throw-in
- when a player may be penalized for being in an offside position
- when a substitution is requested
- when misconduct or any other incident has occurred out of the view of the Referee

ASSISTANCE

The Assistant Referees also assist the Referee to control the match in accordance with the Laws of the Game.

In the event of undue interference or improper conduct, the Referee will relieve an Assistant Referee of his duties and make a report to the appropriate authorities.

LAW 7—THE DURATION OF THE MATCH

PERIODS OF PLAY

The match lasts two equal periods of 45 minutes, unless otherwise mutually agreed between the Referee and the two participating teams. Any agreement to alter the periods of play (for example to reduce each half to 40 minutes because of insufficient light) must be made before the start of play and must comply with competition rules.

HALFTIME INTERVAL

Players are entitled to an interval at halftime.

The halftime interval must not exceed 15 minutes.

Competition rules must state the duration of the halftime interval.

The duration of the halftime interval may be altered only with the consent of the Referee.

ALLOWANCE FOR TIME LOST

Allowance is made in either period for all time lost through:

- *substitution(s)*
- *assessment of injury to players*
- *removal of injured players from the field of play for treatment*
- *wasting time*
- *any other cause*

The allowance for time lost is at the discretion of the Referee.

PENALTY KICK

Additional time is allowed for a penalty kick to be taken at the end of each half or at the end of periods of extra time.

EXTRA TIME

Competition rules may provide for two further equal periods to be played. The conditions of Law 8 will apply.

ABANDONED MATCH

An abandoned match is replayed unless the competition rules provide otherwise.

LAW 8—THE START AND RESTART OF PLAY

PRELIMINARIES

A coin is tossed and the team which wins the toss decides which goal it will attack in the first half of the match.

The other team takes the kickoff to start the match.

The team which wins the toss takes the kickoff to start the second half of the match.

In the second half of the match the teams change ends and attack the opposite goals.

KICKOFF

A kickoff is a way of starting or restarting play:

- *at the start of the match*
- *after a goal has been scored*
- *at the start of the second half of the match*
- *at the start of each period of extra time, where applicable*

A goal may be scored directly from a kickoff.

PROCEDURE

- *all players are in their own half of the field*
- *the opponents of the team taking the kickoff are at least 10 yd. (9.15 m.) from the ball until it is in play*
- *the ball is stationary on the center mark*
- *the Referee gives a signal*
- *the ball is in play when it is kicked and moves forward*
- *the kicker does not touch the ball a second time until it has touched another player*

After a team scores a goal, the kickoff is taken by the other team.

INFRINGEMENTS/SANCTIONS

If the kicker touches the ball a second time before it has touched another player:

- *an indirect free kick is awarded to the opposing team to be taken from the place where the infringement occurred*

For any other infringement of the kickoff procedure:

- *the kickoff is retaken*

DROPPED BALL

A dropped ball is a way of restarting the match after a temporary stoppage which becomes necessary, while the ball is in play, for any reason not mentioned elsewhere in the Laws of the Game.

PROCEDURE

The Referee drops the ball at the place where it was located when play was stopped.*

Play restarts when the ball touches the ground.

INFRINGEMENTS/SANCTIONS

The ball is dropped again:

- *if it is touched by a player before it makes contact with the ground*
- *if the ball leaves the field of play after it makes contact with the ground, without a player touching it*

SPECIAL CIRCUMSTANCES

A free kick awarded to the defending team inside its own goal area is taken from any point within the goal area.

An indirect free kick awarded to the attacking team in its opponents' goal area is taken from the goal area line parallel to the goal line at the point nearest to where the infringement occurrred.

A dropped ball to restart the match after play has been temporarily stopped inside the goal area takes place on the goal area line parallel to the goal line at the point nearest to where the ball was located when play was stopped.

LAW 9—THE BALL IN AND OUT OF PLAY

BALL OUT OF PLAY

The ball is out of play when:
- it has wholly crossed the goal line or touchline whether on the ground or in the air
- play has been stopped by the Referee

BALL IN PLAY

The ball is in play at all other times, including when:
- it rebounds from a goalpost, crossbar, or corner flagpost and remains in the field of play
- it rebounds from either the Referee or an Assistant Referee when they are on the field of play

LAW 10—THE METHOD OF SCORING

GOAL SCORED

A goal is scored when the whole of the ball passes over the goal line, between the goalposts, and under the crossbar, provided that no infringement of the Laws of the Game has been committed previously by the team scoring the goal.

WINNING TEAM

The team scoring the greater number of goals during a match is the winner. If both teams score an equal number of goals, or if no goals are scored, the match is drawn.

COMPETITION RULES

For matches ending in a draw, competition rules may state provisions involving extra time or other procedures approved by the International Football Association Board to determine the winner of the match.

LAW 11—OFFSIDE

OFFSIDE POSITION

It is not an offense in itself to be in an offside position.

A player is in an offside position if:

- *he is nearer to his opponents' goal line than both the ball and the second-to-last opponent*

A player is not in an offside position if:

- *he is in his own half of the field of play* **or**
- *he is level with the second-to-last opponent* **or**
- *he is level with the last two opponents*

OFFENSE

A player in an offside position is only penalized if, at the moment the ball touches or is played by one of his team, he is, in the opinion of the Referee, involved in active play by:

- *interfering with play* **or**
- *interfering with an opponent* **or**
- *gaining an advantage by being in that position*

NO OFFENSE

There is no offside offense if a player receives the ball directly from:

- *a goal kick* **or**
- *a throw-in* **or**
- *a corner kick*

INFRINGEMENTS/SANCTIONS

For any offside offense, the Referee awards an indirect free kick to the opposing team to be taken from the place where the infringement occurred.*

LAW 12—FOULS AND MISCONDUCT

Fouls and misconduct are penalized as follows:

DIRECT FREE KICK

A direct free kick is awarded to the opposing team if a player commits any of the following six offenses in a manner considered by the Referee to be careless, reckless, or using excessive force:

- kicks or attempts to kick an opponent
- trips or attempts to trip an opponent
- jumps at an opponent
- charges at an opponent
- strikes or attempts to strike an opponent
- pushes an opponent

A direct free kick is also awarded to the opposing team if a player commits any of the following four offenses:

- tackles an opponent to gain possession of the ball, making contact with the opponent before touching the ball
- holds an opponent
- spits at an opponent
- handles the ball deliberately (except for the goalkeper within his own penalty area)

A direct free kick is taken from where the offense occurred.*

PENALTY KICK

A penalty kick is awarded if any of the above ten offenses is committed by a player inside his own penalty area, irrespective of the position of the ball, provided it is in play.

INDIRECT FREE KICK

An indirect free kick is awarded to the opposing team if a goalkeeper, inside his own penalty area, commits any of the following five offenses:

- takes more than four steps while controlling the ball with his hands before releasing it from his possession
- touches the ball again with his hands after it has been released from his possession and has not touched any other player
- touches the ball with his hands after it has been deliberately kicked to him by a teammate
- touches the ball with his hands after he has received it directly from a throw-in taken by a teammate
- wastes time

An indirect free kick is also awarded to the opposing team if a player, in the opinion of the Referee:

- *plays in a dangerous manner*
- *impedes the progress of an opponent*
- *prevents the goalkeeper from releasing the ball from his hands*
- *commits any other offense, not previously mentioned in Law 12, for which play is stopped to caution or dismiss a player*

The indirect free kick is taken from where the offense occurred.*

DISCIPLINARY SANCTIONS

CAUTIONABLE OFFENSES

A player is cautioned and shown the yellow card if he commits any of the following seven offenses:

1. *is guilty of unsporting behavior*
2. *shows dissent by word or action*
3. *persistently infringes the Laws of the Game*
4. *delays the restart of play*
5. *fails to respect the required distance when play is restarted with a corner kick or free kick*
6. *enters or reenters the field of play without the Referee's permission*
7. *deliberately leaves the field of play without the Referee's permission*

SENDING-OFF OFFENSES

A player is sent off and shown the red card if he commits any of the following seven offenses:

1. *is guilty of serious foul play*
2. *is guilty of violent conduct*
3. *spits at an opponent or any other person*
4. *denies the opposing team a goal or an obvious goal-scoring opportunity by deliberately handling the ball (this does not apply to a goalkeeper within his own penalty area)*
5. *denies an obvious goal-scoring opportunity to an opponent moving towards the player's goal by an offense punishable by a free kick or a penalty kick*
6. *uses offensive, insulting, or abusive language*
7. *receives a second caution in the same match*

120

DECISIONS OF THE INTERNATIONAL FOOTBALL ASSOCIATION BOARD

● DECISION 1

A penalty kick is awarded if, while the ball is in play, the goal-keeper, inside his own penalty area, strikes or attempts to strike an opponent by throwing the ball at him.

● DECISION 2

A player who commits a cautionable or sending-off offense, either on or off the field of play, whether directed towards an opponent, a teammate, the Referee, an Assistant Referee, or any other person, is disciplined according to the nature of the offense committed.

● DECISION 3

The goalkeeper is considered to be in control of the ball by touching it with any part of his hand or arm. Possession of the ball includes the goalkeeper deliberately parrying the ball, but does not include the circumstances where, in the opinion of the Referee, the ball rebounds accidentally from the goalkeeper, for example after he has made a save.

The goalkeeper is considered to be guilty of time-wasting if he holds the ball in his hands or arms for more than 5-6 seconds.

● DECISION 4

Subject to the term of Law 12, a player may pass the ball to his own goalkeeper using his head or chest or knee, etc. If, however, in the opinion of the Referee, a player uses a deliberate trick while the ball is in play in order to circumvent the Law, the player is guilty of unsporting behavior. He is cautioned, shown the yellow card, and an indirect free kick is awarded to the opposing team from the place where the infringement occurred.*

A player using a deliberate trick to circumvent the Law while he is taking a free kick is cautioned for unsporting behavior and shown the yellow card. The free kick is retaken.

In such circumstances, it is irrelevant whether the goalkeeper subsequently touches the ball with his hands or not. The offense is committed by the player in attempting to circumvent both the letter and the spirit of Law 12.

● DECISION 5

A tackle from behind, which endangers the safety of an opponent, must be sanctioned as serious foul play.

● DECISION 6

Any simulating action anywhere on the field, which is intended to deceive the Referee, must be sanctioned as unsporting behavior.

LAW 13—FREE KICKS

TYPES OF FREE KICKS

Free kicks are either direct or indirect.

For both direct and indirect free kicks, the ball must be stationary when the kick is taken and the kicker does not touch the ball a second time until it has touched another player.

THE DIRECT FREE KICK

- if a direct free kick is kicked directly into the opponents' goal, a goal is awarded
- if a direct free kick is kicked directly into the team's own goal, a corner kick is awarded to the opposing team

THE INDIRECT FREE KICK

SIGNAL The Referee indicates an indirect free kick by raising his arm above his head. He maintains his arm in that position until the kick has been taken and the ball has touched another player or goes out of play.

BALL ENTERS THE GOAL A goal can be scored only if the ball subsequently touches another player before it enters the goal.

- if an indirect free kick is kicked directly into the opponents' goal, a goal kick is awarded
- if an indirect free kick is kicked directly into the team's own goal, a corner kick is awarded to the opposing team

POSITION OF FREE KICK

FREE KICK INSIDE THE PENALTY AREA

Direct or indirect free kick to the defending team:

- all opponents are at least 10 yd. (9.15 m.) from the ball
- all opponents remain outside the penalty area until the ball is in play
- the ball is in play when it is kicked directly beyond the penalty area
- a free kick awarded in the goal area is taken from any point inside that area

INDIRECT FREE KICK TO THE ATTACKING TEAM:

- all opponents are at least 10 yd. (9.15 m.) from the ball until it is in play, unless they are on their own goal line between the goalposts
- the ball is in play when it is kicked and moves
- an indirect free kick awarded inside the goal area is taken from that part of the goal area line which runs parallel to the goal line, at the point nearest to where the infringement occurred

FREE KICK OUTSIDE THE PENALTY AREA
- all opponents are at least 10 yd. (9.15 m.) from the ball until it is in play
- the ball is in play when it is kicked and moves
- the free kick is taken from the place where the infringement occurred

---

INFRINGEMENTS/SANCTIONS
If, when a free kick is taken, an opponent is closer to the ball than the required distance:
- the kick is retaken

If, when a free kick is taken by the defending team from inside its own penalty area, the ball is not kicked directly into play:
- the kick is retaken

FREE KICK TAKEN BY A PLAYER OTHER THAN THE GOALKEEPER

If, after the ball is in play, the kicker touches the ball a second time (except with his hands) before it has touched another player:
- an indirect free kick is awarded to the opposing team, the kick to be taken from the place where the infringement occurred*

123

If, after the ball is in play, the kicker deliberately handles the ball before it has touched another player:
- a direct free kick is awarded to the opposing team, the kick to be taken from the place where the infringement occurred*
- a penalty kick is awarded if the infringement occurred inside the kicker's penalty area

FREE KICK TAKEN BY THE GOALKEEPER

If, after the ball is in play, the goalkeeper touches the ball a second time (except with his hands) before it has touched another player:
- an indirect free kick is awarded to the opposing team, the kick to be taken from the place where the infringement occurred*

If, after the ball is in play, the goalkeeper deliberately handles the ball before it has touched another player:
- a direct free kick is awarded to the opposing team if the infringement occurred outside the goalkeeper's penalty area, the kick to be taken from the place where the infringement occurred*
- an indirect free kick is awarded to the opposing team if the infringement occurred inside the goalkeeper's penalty area, the kick to be taken from the place where the infringement occurrred*

LAW 14—THE PENALTY KICK

A penalty kick is awarded against a team which commits one of the ten offenses for which a direct free kick is awarded, inside its own penalty area and while the ball is in play.

A goal may be scored directly from a penalty kick.

Additional time is allowed for a penalty kick to be taken at the end of each half or at the end of periods of extra time.

POSITION OF THE BALL AND THE PLAYERS

The ball:

- *is placed on the penalty mark*

The player taking the penalty kick:

- *is properly identified*

The defending goalkeeper:

- *remains on his goal line, facing the kicker, between the goalposts until the ball has been kicked*

The players other than the kicker are located:

- *inside the field of play*
- *outside the penalty area*
- *behind the penalty mark*
- *at least 10 yd. (9.15 m.) from the penalty mark*

THE REFEREE

- *does not signal for a penalty kick to be taken until the players have taken up position in accordance with the Law*
- *decides when a penalty kick has been completed*

PROCEDURE

- *the player taking the penalty kicks the ball forward*
- *he does not play the ball a second time until it has touched another player*
- *the ball is in play when it is kicked and moves forward*

When a penalty kick is taken during the normal course of play, or time has been extended at halftime or full time to allow a penalty kick to be taken or retaken, a goal is awarded if, before passing between the goalposts and under the crossbar:

- *the ball touches either or both of the goalposts and/or the crossbar, and/or the goalkeeper*

INFRINGEMENTS/SANCTIONS

If the Referee gives the signal for a penalty kick to be taken and, before the ball is in play, one of the following situations occurs:

The player taking the penalty kick infringes the Laws of the Game:
- *the Referee allows the kick to proceed*
- *if the ball enters the goal, the kick is retaken*
- *if the ball does not enter the goal, the kick is not retaken*

The goalkeeper infringes the Laws of the Game:
- *the Referee allows the kick to proceed*
- *if the ball enters the goal, the goal is awarded*
- *if the ball does not enter the goal, the kick is retaken*

A teammate of the player taking the kick enters the penalty area or moves in front of or within 10 yd. (9.15 m.) of the penalty mark:
- *the Referee allows the kick to proceed*
- *if the ball enters the goal, the kick is retaken*
- *if the ball does not enter the goal, the kick is not retaken*
- *if the ball rebounds from the goalkeeper, the crossbar, or the goalpost and is touched by this player, the Referee stops play and restarts the match with an indirect free kick to the defending team*

A teammate of the goalkeeper enters the penalty area or moves in front of or within 10 yd. (9.15 m.) of the penalty mark:
- *the Referee allows the kick to proceed*
- *if the ball enters the goal, a goal is awarded*
- *if the ball does not enter the goal, the kick is retaken*

A player of both the defending team and the attacking team infringes the Laws of the Game:
- *the kick is retaken*

If, after the penalty kick has been taken:

The kicker touches the ball a second time (except with his hands) before it has touched another player:
- *an indirect free kick is awarded to the opposing team, the kick to be taken from the place where the infringement occurred**

The kicker deliberately handles the ball before it has touched another player:
- *a direct free kick is awarded to the opposing team, the kick to be taken from the place where the infringement occurred**

The ball is touched by an outside agent as it moves forward:
- *the kick is retaken*

The ball rebounds into the field of play from the goalkeeper, the crossbar, or the goalposts, and is then touched by an outside agent:
- *the Referee stops play*
- *play is restarted with a dropped ball at the place where it touched the outside agent**

LAW 15—THE THROW-IN

A throw-in is a method of restarting play.

A goal cannot be scored directly from a throw-in.

A throw-in is awarded:

- *when the whole of the ball passes over the touchline, either on the ground or in the air*
- *from the point where it crossed the touchline*
- *to the opponents of the player who last touched the ball*

PROCEDURE

At the moment of delivering the ball, the thrower:

- *faces the field of play*
- *has part of each foot either on the touchline or on the ground outside the touchline*
- *uses both hands*
- *delivers the ball from behind and over his head*

The thrower may not touch the ball again until it has touched another player.

The ball is in play immediately when it enters the field of play.

INFRINGEMENTS/SANCTIONS

THROW-IN TAKEN BY A PLAYER OTHER THAN THE GOALKEEPER

If, after the the ball is in play, the thrower touches the ball a second time (except with his hands) before it has touched another player:

- *an indirect free kick is awarded to the opposing team, the kick to be taken from the place where the infringement occurred**

If, after the ball is in play, the thrower deliberately handles the ball before it has touched another player:

- *a direct free kick is awarded to the opposing team, the kick to be taken from the place where the infringement occurred**
- *a penalty kick is awarded if the infringement occurred inside the thrower's penalty area*

THROW-IN TAKEN BY THE GOALKEEPER

If, after the ball is in play, the goalkeeper touches the ball a second time (except with his hands), before it has touched another player:

- *an indirect free kick is awarded to the opposing team, the kick to be taken from the place where the infringement occurred**

If, after the ball is in play, the goalkeeper deliberately handles the ball before it has touched another player:

- *a direct free kick is awarded to the opposing team if the infringement occurred outside the goalkeeper's penalty area, the kick to be taken from the place where the infringement occurred**
- *an indirect free kick is awarded to the opposing team if the infringement occurred inside the goalkeeper's penalty area, the kick to be taken from the place where the infringement occurred**

If an opponent unfairly distracts or impedes the thrower:

- *he is cautioned for unsporting behavior and shown the yellow card*

For any other infringement of this Law:

- *the throw-in is taken by a player of the opposing team*

LAW 16—THE GOAL KICK

A goal kick is a method of restarting play.

A goal may be scored directly from a goal kick, but only against the opposing team.

A goal kick is awarded when:

- the whole of the ball, having last touched a player of the attacking team, passes over the goal line, either on the ground or in the air, and a goal is not scored in accordance with Law 10

PROCEDURE

- the ball is kicked from any point within the goal area by a player of the defending team
- opponents remain outside the penalty area until the ball is in play
- the kicker does not play the ball a second time until it has touched another player
- the ball is in play when it is kicked directly beyond the penalty area

INFRINGEMENTS/SANCTIONS

If the ball is not kicked directly into play beyond the penalty area:
- the kick is retaken

GOAL KICK TAKEN BY A PLAYER OTHER THAN THE GOALKEEPER

If, after the ball is in play, the kicker touches the ball a second time (except with his hands) before it has touched another player:

- an indirect free kick is awarded to the opposing team, the kick to be taken from the place where the infringement occurred*

If, after the ball is in play, the kicker deliberately handles the ball before it has touched another player:

- a direct free kick is awarded to the opposing team, the kick to be taken from the place where the infringement occurred*
- a penalty kick is awarded if the infringement occurred inside the kicker's penalty area

GOAL KICK TAKEN BY THE GOALKEEPER

If, after the ball is in play, the goalkeeper touches the ball a second time (except with his hands) before it has touched another player:

- an indirect free kick is awarded to the opposing team, the kick to be taken from the place where the infringement occurred*

If, after the ball is in play, the goalkeeper deliberately handles the ball before it has touched another player:

- a direct free kick is awarded to the opposing team if the infringement occurred outside the goalkeeper's penalty area, the kick to be taken from the place where the infringement occurred*
- an indirect free kick is awarded to the opposing team if the infringement occurred inside the goalkeeper's penalty area, the kick to be taken from the place where the infringement occurred*

For any other infringement of this Law:
- the kick is retaken

LAW 17—THE CORNER KICK

A corner kick is a method of restarting play.

A goal may be scored directly from a corner kick, but only against the opposing team.

A corner kick is awarded when:

- *the whole of the ball, having last touched a player of the defending team, passes over the goal line, either on the ground or in the air, and a goal is not scored in accordance with Law 10.*

PROCEDURE

- *the ball is placed inside the corner arc at the nearest corner flagpost*
- *the corner flagpost is not moved*
- *opponents remain at least 10 yd. (9.15 m.) from the ball until it is in play*
- *the ball is kicked by a player of the attacking team*
- *the ball is in play when it is kicked and moves*
- *the kicker does not play the ball a second time until it has touched another player*

INFRINGEMENTS/SANCTIONS

CORNER KICK TAKEN BY A PLAYER OTHER THAN THE GOALKEEPER

If, after the ball is in play, the kicker touches the ball a second time (except with his hands) before it has touched another player:

- *an indirect free kick is awarded to the opposing team, the kick to be taken from the place where the infringement occurred**

If, after the ball is in play, the kicker deliberately handles the ball before it has touched another player:

- *a direct free kick is awarded to the opposing team, the kick to be taken from the place where the infringement occurred**
- *a penalty kick is awarded if the infringement occurred inside the kicker's penalty area*

CORNER KICK TAKEN BY THE GOALKEEPER

If, after the ball is in play, the goalkeeper touches the ball a second time (except with his hands) before it has touched another player:

- *an indirect free kick is awarded to the opposing team, the kick to be taken from the place where the infringement occurred**

If, after the ball is in play, the goalkeeper deliberately handles the ball before it has touched another player:

- *a direct free kick is awarded to the opposing team if the infringement occurred outside the goal-keeper's penalty area, the kick to be taken from the place where the infringement occurred**
- *an indirect free kick is awarded to the opposing team if the infringement occurred inside the goalkeeper's penalty area, the kick to be taken from the place where the infringement occurred**

For any other infringement of this Law:

- *the kick is retaken*

SECTION 8

THE FINAL WHISTLE

EXTRA INFORMATION

MATCH DECIDERS

FOR KNOCK-OUT COMPETITIONS

Match deciders or **tie-breakers** came into soccer in 1970 to replace the unsatisfactory method of deciding tied matches, in knock-out competitions, by the toss of a coin. The system adopted by the International F. A. Board was a series of kicks from the penalty mark. The official procedure is set out below.

KICKS FROM THE PENALTY MARK

Taking kicks from the penalty mark is a method of determining the winning team where competition rules require there to be a winning team after a match has been drawn.

PROCEDURE

- the Referee chooses the goal at which the kicks will be taken
- the Referee tosses a coin and the team whose captain wins the toss takes the first kick
- the Referee keeps a record of the kicks being taken
- subject to the conditions explained below, both teams take five kicks
- the kicks are taken alternately by the teams
- if, before both teams have taken five kicks, one has scored more goals than the other could score, even if it were to complete its five kicks, no more kicks are taken
- if, after both teams have taken five kicks, both have scored the same number of goals, or have not scored any goals, kicks continue to be taken in the same order until one team has scored a goal more than the other from the same number of kicks
- a goalkeeper who is injured while kicks are being taken from the penalty mark and is unable to continue as goalkeeper may be replaced by a named substitute provided his team has not used the maximum number of substitutes permitted under the competition rules
- with the exception of the foregoing case, only players who are on the field of play at the end of the match, which includes extra time where appropriate, are allowed to take kicks from the penalty mark
- each kick is taken by a different player and all eligible players must take a kick before any player can take a second kick
- an eligible player may change places with the goalkeeper at any time when kicks from the penalty mark are being taken
- only the eligible players and match officials are permitted to remain on the field of play when kicks from the penalty mark are being taken
- all players, except the player taking the kick and the two goalkeepers, must remain within the center circle
- the goalkeeper who is the teammate of the kicker must remain on the field of play, outside the penalty area in which the kicks are being taken, on the goal line where it meets the penalty area boundary line
- unless otherwise stated, the relevant Laws of the Game and International F. A. Board apply when kicks from the penalty marks are being taken

THE TECHNICAL AREA

When the role of the Coach was formally recognized in 1993 it became necessary to define the location where tactical instructions could be given. This was named the **technical area.** Televised soccer usually shows this area as where the substitutes are seated.

The official description of the area and its use are quoted below.

The technical area described in Law 3, International F. A. Board Decision no. 2, relates particularly to matches played in stadia with a designated seated area for technical staff and substitutes.

Technical areas may vary between stadia, for example in size or location, and the following notes are issued for general guidance:

- the technical area extends 1 yd. (1 m.) on either side of the designated seated area and extends forward up to a distance of 1 yd. (1 m.) from the touchline
- it is recommended that markings are used to define this area
- the number of persons permitted to occupy the technical area is defined by the competition rules
- the occupants of the technical area are identified before the beginning of the match in accordance with the competition rules
- only one person at a time is authorized to convey tactical instruction and he must return to his position immediately after giving these instructions
- the coach and other officials must remain within the confines of the technical area except in special circumstances, such as a physiotherapist or doctor entering the field of play, with the Referee's permission, to assess an injured player
- the coach and other occupants of the technical area must behave in a responsible manner

133

THE FOURTH OFFICIAL

A fourth match official was originally required as a standby Referee, available to take over the duties of either the appointed Referee or one of the Assistant Referees in case of injury or illness.

The fourth official is now required to undertake a range of duties to ease the tasks of his three match colleagues. The role has become important in high level soccer as can be seen in the following description of duties and responsibilities:

- the fourth official may be appointed under the competition rules and officiates if any of the three match officials are unable to continue
- prior to the start of the competition, the organizer states clearly whether, if the Referee is unable to continue, the fourth official takes over as the Match Referee or whether the senior Assistant Referee takes over as Referee with the fourth official becoming an Assistant Referee
- the fourth official assists with any administrative duties before, during, and after the match, as required by the Referee
- he is responsible for assisting with substitution procedures during the match
- he supervises the replacement soccer balls, where required. If the match ball has to be replaced during a match, he provides another ball, on the instruction of the Referee, thus keeping the delay to a minimum
- he has the authority to check the equipment of substitutes before they enter the field of play. If their equipment does not comply with the Laws of the Game, he informs the Referee
- he has the authority to inform the Referee of irresponsible behavior by any occupant of the technical area
- after the match, the fourth official must submit a report to the appropriate authorities on any misconduct or other incident which has occurred out of the view of the Referee and the Assistant Referees. The fourth official must advise the Referee and his assistants of any report being made.